A
FAREWELL
to the
KING

A
FAREWELL
to the
KING

A Personal Look Back
at the Career of
Richard Petty,
Stock Car Racing's
Winningest and
Most Popular Driver

Frank Vehorn

ISBN Number
1-878086-12-X

Library of Congress Catalog Card Number
92-071495

Printed in the United States of America

Cover and book design
by Elizabeth House

Cover photographs
by Jerry Haislip

Inside photographs
from the author's personal collection

Down Home Press
P.O. Box 4126
Asheboro, N.C. 27204

For my Petty fans

Esther, Bill, Steven, and Andrew.

CONTENTS

FOREWORD

Once upon a time, Richard Petty rode only the high, fast lanes of the NASCAR Winston Cup circuit. His bright, wide smile was as common in victory lanes as good-looking beauty queens and champagne.

There was not a race he hadn't won, back in the days when they raced more often under a cloud of dust at such stops as Columbia Speedway than on the high-banked ribbons of superfast asphalt.

He was "King Richard," and when he cranked Ol' 43 to life and rolled to the starting line, everyone knew he was the man to beat.

Richard Petty became the biggest hero in Dixie, and eventually his popularity spread around the world. He had fan clubs behind the Iron Curtain. During the 1967 season when he was rolling to 27 victories, a newspaper in the Yukon ran a story under the headline "Petty Finishes Second." It didn't seem to matter who was first, if it were not Richard.

Fan mail from across the oceans, addressed only to "Richard Petty, USA," found its way to the small rural post office in Level Cross, N.C.

During those glory days little boys with STP decals on their bicycles raced down the back alleys of mill villages with their mommas cheering them on.

A kid couldn't have a better hero. There never was a more accommodating superstar, or one who filled the role so splendidly. Wide-brimmed cowboy hats, dark glasses, silver belt-buckles, boots, and a fancy signature were his trademarks.

For so many splendid seasons on the stock car tour that stretched from coast-to-coast, Richard's life seemed to be a nonstop joy ride from one checkered flag to another.

We thought the moon would lose its glow, and the Mississippi River would run dry before Richard Petty stopped winning races.

But, as we come to sadly learn, nothing lasts forever.

The man who once couldn't lose for winning suddenly couldn't win for losing. The steady stream of victories became a trickle, and then sputtered dry.

A new generation of heroes sped onto the scene. Drivers like Dale Earnhardt and Darrell Waltrip, Bill Elliott and Rusty Wallace. What never changed, though, was Richard Petty's status as king of NASCAR.

When Richard began the 1992 season, which would conclude his driving career, he had not won a race since posting his 200th career victory in 1984. Yet, he still had the respect of his peers and the admiration of his fans.

"Anyone would be foolish to think Richard can't still win races, or even get on a roll and end his career by winning another championship. I still see the fire in his eyes, that determination to win. He is still the King, and always will be, as far as I am concerned," Earnhardt said.

Cranking up what Richard had proclaimed as his "Fan Appreciation Tour," the 1992 Daytona 500 became a special tribute to racing's most famous superstar. Fans came from every state and several foreign countries, hoping to see him win one more Daytona 500, but willing to settle for just the thrill of watching the King make his final high-speed ride in stock car racing's grand event.

The "Ten Days of Daytona" were engulfed in a carnival atmosphere.

Visitors to the garage area sought out Richard's red and blue Pontiac and inspected it with awe and respect, as they would any other national monument. Those not fortunate enough to get into the Daytona garage area for an upclose glimpse of the King and his chariot lined up by the thousands to get a snapshot and an autograph at his many personal appearances away from the track.

There was a Richard Petty look-a-like contest one night. Richard bowled for charity and auctioned off his cowboy hat for $1,200 on another night. He toured the numerous radio talk shows, fielding questions from callers through-out the nation. He patiently answered the same, old questions from the media and never once complained or frowned.

Wherever Richard went, he seemed to be towing a crowd of television cameramen, photographers, reporters, and just plain fans with him. As he always had, Richard made time to give to the fans, the media, and the numerous sponsors he represented.

That was one of the reasons for him giving the sport a one-year notice of his retirement as a driver instead of just crawling out of the car one day and saying, "That's it, no more," as he once thought he might do. "I didn't want anyone coming up to me later on and saying 'you never gave me a chance to see you race one more time' " Richard explained.

He stressed, too, that this was not a farewell tour because he would be only changing roles and not retiring from the circuit. He'd be back for the next Daytona 500, and the next season, as a car owner.

For now, he was still a driver and, like Earnhardt, I could see he had not come into this final season just for the ride.

Richard was determined to go out a winner.

He would do that if he made it back to victory lane one more time or not. He already had given us hundreds of victories and a lifetime of fond memories.

The memories we treasure the most.

LITTLE RICHARD

Richard Petty says his first race was no big deal, and I have to believe him. At the time Richard began his driving career at the old half-mile dirt track at Columbia, S.C., I was still in high school in Cheraw, S.C., about 80 miles away and don't remember anything being said about it. Of course, in those days, stock car racing did not receive much media attention, but that would change. By the time Richard began his final season as a driver at the 1992 Daytona 500, more than a thousand reporters and photographers would show up to record the event.

It was four years after Richard's debut that I began my career as a motorsports journalist, appropriately enough, at the same half-mile Columbia Speedway, where Thursday-night heroes in those days included Tiny Lund, LeeRoy Yarbrough, Little Bud Moore, Ralph Earnhardt, and Cale Yarborough.

The big show, the Grand National circuit which is now called Winston Cup, visited Columbia twice a year, and it was in the summer

There wasn't a formal announcement that Lee Petty's oldest boy was going to start his racing career. He just showed up for it, the way they did in those days.

of 1962 that I met Richard for the first time. I forgive him for forgetting. I don't remember much about that first race either. He had won a few races by then, but he was not yet King Richard.

The nickname I remember fans and others in the pits calling him was "Little Richard." Not because of his size – he already was over six feet tall – but because everyone had known him for years as Lee Petty's little boy.

What I remember most was seeing Richard's brother, Maurice, spin out a couple of times while warming up for the 200-lapper.

Maurice's talent was with wrenches, not the steering wheel. He became one of the sport's greatest mechanics, and built the engines that powered Richard to most of his 200 victories and all seven of his Winston Cup championships.

Ironically, Richard once told me, he initially wanted to be a mechanic, too. That was when he was too young to drive and it seemed the only way for him to travel to the tracks with his father.

That all changed, though, when Richard got his first real taste of driving. That was in a NASCAR convertible race at the Columbia track in 1958. I have talked to Richard about that first race many times, and I have read and heard other first-hand reports about it.

There wasn't a formal announcement that Lee Petty's oldest boy was going to start his racing career. He just showed up for it, the way they did in those days.

Here is the way Richard described that first race to me:

"I had told Daddy a couple of years before that I wanted to race, and he told me I would have to wait until I was twenty-one. We really didn't talk much about it again until right after I turned twenty-one. Daddy was going to run a Grand National in Asheville, and there was a convertible race in Columbia on the same night. Normally, we would just pick up a driver to run the convertible car when there were two races on the same night. But I told Daddy he ought to let me drive the car, since I was twenty-one, instead of going out and looking for someone else."

For whatever reason, Lee agreed, despite Richard having virtually no experience on a race track, and none at all in an actual race.

"We had an old dirt test track out behind our house that Daddy would test stuff on," Richard said. "I had driven on it some, and one day when Daddy was testing a new four-barrel carburetor he got tired and I asked him to let me drive some. I went a few laps and then spun out and landed in the woods. That was the end of that."

Richard recruited his cousin, Dale Inman, and Ken (Red) Myler to be his crew for the Columbia race. His biggest concern was that the race was a 200-lapper and he did not know if he had the stamina to go the distance. Most people start out in 25- or 50-lap events.

"I didn't know if I could drive 200 laps or not, so I told Dale if some other driver dropped out early to bring him to our pits in case I needed relief," Richard said, pausing to laugh.

"Joe Weatherly dropped out early and Dale asked him to come to our pit to stand by. About halfway through the race my head started itching. I guess it was because the weather was so hot, and I wasn't used to the driver's helmet that I was wearing.

"Every other lap I would try to scratch my head, but I was really scratching the helmet. Dale and Joe thought I was indicating I was coming in for relief, so Joe would put on his driving gloves and helmet and get ready.

"I wouldn't come in, though. Joe would take the helmet and gloves off and stand by. Then, I would scratch my helmet again, and Joe would put his gear back on. That kept happening until finally Joe got mad and walked away."

Richard remembers that someone wrecked in front of him and crashed through the outside wood-board fence. "There was all of this wood and debris flying up in front of me, and a piece of it hit my helmet. I let go of the steering wheel and threw my hands up in front of my face," he said. "I don't know why I didn't wreck."

Another thing that he remembers doing from the first lap on was driving into the turn low and coming out high, straight toward the fence, and at the last moment jerking the steering wheel down. It became his style of racing.

"Nobody else drove that way, but that is how I started to drive, and I just kept driving that way," he said.

I wondered why Richard had not attempted to imitate the style of his father, or any of the other great drivers of that day, such as Fireball Roberts or Weatherly. "Well," he replied, "you have to remember I was not trying to win that first race. I just wanted to finish and I was looking for a driving style that would be comfortable for me."

His style was good enough to finish sixth, although six laps down to winner Bob Welborn, but Petty was a happy young man on the trip back home to Level Cross. "I thought I really had done something," Richard said. "But I was so cocky from that first race that I think I wrecked in my next three races."

The next race for him was in Toronto, Ontario, which really was his first start on NASCAR's premier circuit. He then drove in races at Buffalo, N.Y., Belmar, N.J., and at Bowman-Gray Stadium, a little oval built around a football field, in Winston-Salem, N.C. Since it was just up the road from Level Cross, a lot of his friends were there for the first time to see him race.

"I spun out about seven times," he recalled. "I spent more time on the football field than I did the race track."

I was curious about how much money Richard, who would become NASCAR's first $1-million driver, won in his first race, and how much of it he got to keep.

"It was about $200," he said.

"Before I drove in that first race, Daddy asked me if I wanted to drive for a salary or a percentage of what I won. I wasn't dumb. I told him a salary. He wasn't dumb, either. He signed me to a lifetime contract."

Richard told me that after his first race, he never had any doubts about what he would be doing the rest of his life. He was going to be a race driver.

"Of course, I did not have any idea I would have the success I have had," he added. "Daddy had told me not to expect to win right away, and I didn't. I just wanted to finish in the top ten. Then, after I got to running pretty good, I wanted to win. It was a gradual process. My first victory came on the old dirt track at Charlotte, in 1960. I guess by then I knew I was going to be driver and, by that, I mean a good one."

Richard won two other races in 1960, at Martinsville, Va., and Hillsborough, N.C., and finished second in the Rebel 300 at Darlington, S.C.

By that time, everyone else in racing was realizing that he was going to be a good driver, too.

By that, I mean a great one.

Lee Petty was the tour's winningest and most popular driver before being replaced by his son.

POPPA LEE

Stock car racing once had the reputation for being a rough and rowdy sport in which most competitors were former moonshiners and a man had to be as good at fighting as he was at wrestling a steering wheel to be a survivor.

Needless to say, Lee Petty survived.

I am told by some people who rubbed a few fenders with the man that he may have been the most ruthless driver ever to grip a steering wheel. They say, too, that he was an accomplished diplomat outside of the car — mean enough to run over a few people to get to the checkered flag and smooth enough to talk his way out of a confrontation if someone came looking for a fight.

Lee's competitive spirit didn't just rub off on Richard. It was banged into him. Richard tells the story of the first race he ran with his father. Richard remembers Cotton Owens coming up and passing him smoothly. Hot in pursuit, Lee came up and knocked his own son out of the way.

Before Richard won the hearts of race fans, Poppa Lee was the most popular driver in NASCAR racing. Lee was picked by the fans as the most popular driver on the circuit for three straight years.

Then there is the legendary story about Richard taking the checkered flag for the first time, in a 1959 race in Atlanta. There was a protest, a recheck of the scoring cards, and the victory was snatched from Richard.

The winner was the man who lodged the protest, Lee Petty.

"When the boy earns a victory he can have it. Not before," Lee explained gruffly.

Lee didn't lose that gruffness or competitiveness when he retired, leaving the driving to Richard, and taking up golf. He built his own green out in his front yard and within a couple of years was among the very best amateurs in the state of North Carolina.

He was with golf as he was with driving. He didn't know how to just play just for fun. If anyone was keeping score, he wanted to win.

I remember playing in a foursome behind Lee at a media day event hosted by Martinsville Speedway. It doesn't matter if you don't play that well, just come on out and have some fun, track publicist Dick Thompson told me.

I am eternally thankful that I just missed being included in Lee's foursome.

He clearly was upset when I came off the course.

"How'd you play?" I asked.

"Oh, okay," Lee answered. "But we had this guy playing with us who had a score of 110. They ought not allowed people like that to play."

I gulped silently and nodded. "I know what you mean," I agreed. "We had this guy in our foursome that shot even worse than that."

I didn't tell him that guy was me.

Off the golf course and out of a race car, though, Lee Petty was one of the most likable persons I ever met in racing. He had a great sense of humor and uncomplicated wisdom that he passed on to sons Richard and Maurice.

While Lee did not care to talk about himself much after he got out of racing, I enjoyed two lengthy conversations with him: once before his induction into the North Carolina Sports Hall of Fame, and the other before his induction into the National Motorsports Press Association Hall of Fame at Darlington.

The North Carolina induction came first, in 1966, and was special since Lee was the first motorsports personality admitted. It was significant because some critics said drivers were not legitimate athletes and did not belong in the Hall.

"Anyone who says that has never driven a race car," said Lee, who played football, basketball and baseball as a youth. "It takes just as much stamina, ability, and training to drive a race car as it does to compete in any other sport."

Lee got into racing as a hobby and learned that he could make money doing it. But it didn't happen right away. In his first race he rolled the family Buick four times. "Actually," he corrected, "the car was owned jointly by the family and the finance company."

Lee won national championships in 1954, 1958 and 1959, and held the record until Richard broke it. He won 54 career races, another record that his son reset.

Before Richard won the hearts of race fans, Poppa Lee was the most popular driver in NASCAR racing. Lee was picked by the fans as the most popular driver on the circuit for three straight years, prompting the rules to be changed to give others a chance.

Lee was elected into the Motorsports Hall of Fame by an overwhelming vote the first year he became eligible, in 1969, five years after driving in his final race. He hadn't been seen much around race tracks after he quit driving and discovered golf. But he arrived in Darlington three days early for his induction into the Hall of Fame, time enough for the memories to come swooping back.

"There are no regrets that I have about my career," he told me. "But if there is one place where I wish I had won a race and didn't, well, it would be right here at Darlington."

Lee did not begin racing until he was 35, an age when athletes in most other sports are heading for retirement. His first race was in Greensboro, N.C., in 1947, two years before NASCAR was formed by Bill France, Sr.

The biggest thrill of his career, he said, was winning the inaugural Daytona 500 in 1959.

The photo-finish victory – Lee wasn't declared the official winner until three days later – was the first of many Petty triumphs on the high banks of the two-and-a-half mile speedway.

In the inaugural Southern 500 at Darlington, in 1950, Lee raced a car that he drove off the street.

"We didn't have roll bars in race cars until 1953. I guess I was the first to use them. I was driving a Dodge hardtop and the only reason I put them in was to keep the top from caving in," he said.

Lee was proud of his accomplishments and contributions to racing, but he talked more enthusiastically about Richard's accomplishments than his own.

"You know, I have got a house full of trophies," he said with a grin. "But nothing like Richard has. His attic and basement are full and now he is putting them in our office."

Lee said there was never a big plan for Richard to become a driver, much less the most successful in stock car racing history.

"He just fit right in," Lee said. "I knew he would be a great driver, though. He had the determination and finished well in the first race he drove."

When I talked to Richard on the eve of his father's induction, he said there was only one way to describe has daddy: "He was a winner."

"Daddy didn't give me much advice when I began," Richard said. "He told me to start at the top, which then was the Grand National division, and he'd build me a car. When I was 25, I was already a seasoned veteran while others were just beginning their careers at that age.

"As far as driving the car, the main thing he told me was to drive the car the way I felt like it. He said when I went into the turns to go in as deep as I felt I could and not to listen to what others said. That is the way I have always driven."

Richard recalled the day at Daytona in 1961 when Lee's car sailed over the guard railing. Lee injured his leg in the accident and several operations left him with a permanent limp.

"It was ironic," Richard said. "There were two races that day. I went over the wall in the first race. Daddy tried to get me to drive his car in the second race. He told me he had heard if a driver ever wrecked the best thing he could do was get back on the track and prove he could still drive.

"I told him it was his car, for him to drive it. Then he went out and someone hit him from behind to put him through the fence."

Lee came back to drive in a few more races, just so he could say he quit on his own terms.

"I just lost my ambition to win, and it was time to quit," Lee told me. "Then, too, there was Richard coming on so strong that it made it easier for me to quit driving."

On that Saturday night that Lee was inducted into the Motorsports Hall of Fame, Richard was at home in Level Cross.

"The whole family is just as proud as we can be," Richard explained to me before he left the track to drive home. "But this day belongs to Daddy, and I would not want to distract from that one bit. That is the way we Pettys do things. Daddy was a winner, and he deserves all of the attention."

TRADITIONS

A popular game among sports trivia buffs is to call out a number, any number from 1 to 99, and have someone identify it with a great athlete.

Number 23!

Ah, an easy one. Michael Jordan, of course.

Number 24!

Say, hey. Willie Mays.

In one such list in a national sports publication, only one racing personality was included.

There was no question about who was Number 43. It is the personal trademark of Richard Petty, and has been since his first NASCAR Grand National race. He never signs an autograph without ending it with the number.

But, say-hey Willie Mays, it would have been Number 24, if Richard had gotten his first wish.

"Daddy's race cars were Number 42, and we wanted to use Number 24 for my cars," Richard explained when I asked how he had selected Number 43. "But when we asked NASCAR for

Number 43. It is the personal trademark of Richard Petty, and has been since his first NASCAR Grand National race. He never signs an autograph without ending it with the number.

car Number 24, we were told that someone already was using it. Our second choice was 43."

I can't imagine Richard Petty driving Number 24, or a car with any other number on it, but it did happen once during his career.

That was in 1980 when his son Kyle was beginning his career by driving a car out of Petty Enterprises. Richard decided he would let Kyle drive the car with Number 43 on it since it was on NASCAR's rich Winner's Circle plan, which rewarded car owners who had posted victories.

Richard figured he would drive the Petty car Number 44, win a race, and thus have both cars on the Winner's Circle. Kyle drove Number 43 and Richard drove 44 in the season-opener at Riverside, Calif., but it lasted only one race.

The second race was the nationally-televised Daytona 500, and all of team sponsor STP's pre-race advertisement and promotion had centered around Richard driving Number 43.

Richard went back to his own number and stuck with it for the remainder of his career.

At one time, I and most race fans never believed we would see Richard driving a car that wasn't painted a light blue with white numerals. We called the color "Petty blue" and it came into being just as coincidentally as the number 43.

"We were going to a race and we didn't have enough blue paint for both cars," Richard explained. "So we just mixed in enough white paint to do the job, and that is how it came out."

During Richard's triumphant tour of the 1960s, both he and his race car were known to fans and other competitors simply as "Ol' Blue."

That changed in 1972 when STP negotiated a contract to sponsor the Petty car. STP, already well known for its sponsorships in other types of motorsports, had wanted its name on the side of Richard's car for a couple of years.

But STP kept insisting that Richard paint his cars day-glow red, a trademark of the company's racing program.

The deal was lucrative, but the Pettys stubbornly refused to give up the color by which their race car was known to thousands of fans. Andy Granatelli, the STP boss at the time, was just as stubborn during a meeting between the two parties in Chicago just before the first race of the 1972 season.

Granatelli remembered that ideas such as blue chevrons, or slashes of red paint, and vice versa, were discussed. Never had he seen such stubborn negotiators as the Pettys, he told me.

"We discussed all manner of paint combinations and compromises, but basically I wanted a red car and they wanted a blue one," Granatelli said.

They even talked about painting Richard's car blue for one race, red for the next. They figured the weight build up on the car over a season made that plan impractical.

Richard finally decided there was not any way the two parties could agree. He started to walk out of the discussions when Granatelli and lawyers called him back.

The final compromise was to paint the lower half of the Petty Plymouth red and the upper half blue. "That symbolically put the Petty blue color on top," Granatelli said. "It seemed appropriate since we figured Richard's car would be on top through most of the season."

Granatelli also got in the the last word. He added a clause to the contract saying if Petty should ever agree to paint his race car red all over that he would receive an extra $50,000.

The Pettys never collected.

"No way was I going to do that," Richard said. "I had raced too long with a blue car. Take that away, I would have had to start all over, as far as building an identification with the fans."

Richard says he is not superstitious, but who knows in what direction his career would have turned if he had sold out Ol' Blue?

As it was, Richard quickly learned that a little STP red didn't slow the car at all. He debuted the new paint scheme by winning the race at Riverside, Calif., on Jan. 23, 1972.

The compromise settlement proved rewarding for Richard and STP and resulted in the longest continuous team sponsorship in motorsports history.

The only thing that concerned fans when Richard announced he was going to retire as a driver and continue to field his own race team out of Petty Enterprises was what would happen to Number 43 and the familiar red-and-blue color scheme.

Richard explained the only change would be the driver – not the color, sponsorship, or number, although most fans had hoped Number 43 would be retired in honor of Petty's accomplishments.

NASCAR, which never before had permanently retired a number, seemed willing to do it this time. It was Richard who wanted to keep the number going, even if he was retiring.

Richard knew there was a winning magic in Number 43 that he wanted to take with him as a car owner.

I know that to be true, based on a conversation that I had with Richard following North Carolina State's basketball championship in 1983. I covered the Final Four tournament in which the Wolfpack won the title at the last second when Lorenzo Charles leaped to take a teammate's shot that was falling short and deposited it through the goal for the victory.

At the next race, I dropped by Richard's truck to discuss the game, since I knew he enjoyed following Atlantic Coast Conference teams.

"I knew Charles was going to get that winning basket," Richard told me.

"How's that?" I asked, remembering that Charles' move had surprised everyone watching the game in the arena.

"He was wearing number 43, wasn't he?" Richard replied.

MILLION-DOLLAR MAN

Along the stretch of asphalt that is Route 220, winding southward from Greensboro through the green North Carolina countryside, folks around Randleman and Level Cross once had standard instructions for directing visitors to Petty Enterprises.

"Jes' keep goin' down this here road 'til you get to the crossroads," one was told. "Then roll down your windows and follow the noise of them racin' engines. That will take you right there."

The directions were splendidly adequate during the days that engines in the Petty compound beckoned loud and clear. But in the summer of 1971 it seemed to me that someone should erect a huge dollar sign to mark the location.

With his 134th career victory on a warm Sunday at Atlanta International Raceway, Richard became the first stock car driver to earn a million dollars from race purse winnings. But the historic milestone was not the realization of a predetermined goal by Petty, who, at 34, was unwilling to admit to having any goal other than

With his 134th career victory, Richard Petty became the first stock car driver to earn a million dollars from race purse winnings.

winning the next race, no matter if it was the South Boston 100 or the Daytona 500.

Indeed, in his colorful Carolina style of making his point, Petty told me he could not understand why the media and promoters were making such a big deal of him becoming racing's first million-dollar driver.

"Everyone seems to be counting the money except me," Richard said. "I am not worried about it. Heck, I have already spent that money. I am more concerned with making the next million."

Of course, when Lee Petty began the family team, he was more concerned about making just the next dollar – not a million of them. Richard didn't even count the dollars when he started racing. He was having such a great time that it didn't seem right that a man could make a lot of money out of racing.

"Did I ever think I would win a million dollars when I started?" he said, repeating a question I had asked. "Man, I didn't even know there

During the 1971 season, Richard Petty became the first driver to pass the million-dollar mark in career earnings.

was that much money in the world when I started out. All I wanted to do was race, and keep racing as long as Daddy could pay the bills. Money was no object, not then."

But with the money rolling in, Richard was determined not to permit it to change his outlook. "My enthusiasm for racing is just as great now, maybe even more so, as it was the first time I ever got in a race car. Maybe the emphasis is a little different, though. When you get on top, it is staying there that matters. Once you are a winner you have to work harder to stay that way because everyone wants to knock you off."

It was plainly evident that success was not going to change Richard Petty, or separate him from other drivers who had to struggle to stay in business. At race tracks, the Petty truck was always open to independent drivers who dropped by for a drink of water or a spare part. The only trace of jealousy from some drivers was the huge amount of attention Richard was receiving from the media and fans.

But, just as with his million dollars, Richard had earned the popularity. Always he was available for interviews, autographs, or just to exchange quips with race fans.

At a race in Beltsville, Md., Petty blew an engine early and parked his car at the entrance to the garage area. A fan wandered out of the infield while no one was paying attention and jumped into the Petty car.

He emulated the sound of the engine and jerked the steering wheel as though he was making laps in the race.

"Unnnnnn...un...unnnnnnh," he said as he twisted the steering wheel.

A Petty crewmen saw what was happening and began moving toward the car to ask the fan to get out.

Richard shook his head and signaled for the crewman to stop.

"That cat is having a ball," Richard said.

Although Richard was on top of the racing world, perched there on a stack of dollar bills, he never put himself above the fans or other drivers.

"There is not, and never will be another like him," said Bill Champion, who raced against thousands of drivers during his career. "Richard is as straight as he can be, and nothing ever changes him."

Certainly, his first million dollars in purse winnings didn't.

After all, he explained, it probably took $2 million from the factories and sponsors to win that $1 million.

DAYTONA

The first time Richard Petty saw Daytona International Speedway he thought it looked as big as the state of North Carolina.

That was in 1959, Richard's first full season on the NASCAR tour, and the year the big two-and-a-half mile, high-banked speedway built by NASCAR founder Bill France opened for business.

When Richard arrived to compete in his final Daytona 500 in 1992, he couldn't help but look back through the years and make a comparison to how it was at the beginning.

"I came through the tunnel in 1959 and there was nothing really here," he said. "There was a rope out there, no building and no fences. They had a guard rail around the track and some grandstands. The race track itself was humongous."

None of the drivers had ever raced on such a track and none knew what to expect. NASCAR officials told them to stay on the flat part of the track for the first three or four practice laps, just

By 1981, Daytona Beach had outgrown the laid-back atmosphere that Richard knew years earlier when only racers came to town to strut their stuff.

to get the feel of it.

But the high-banks were just too tempting for an excited 21-year-old kid from rural North Carolina just beginning his racing career. Richard stayed low until he got through the first turn and then steered his car up on the big banks.

"They black-flagged me on my first lap around the place," Richard said with a laugh.

Everyone else had forgotten that Richard's career at Daytona began with a black flag. What we remembered most were all the checkered flags that had waved for him and other Pettys over the years.

Lee Petty won the first Daytona 500, although he did not receive the trophy in Victory Lane. It took three days of studying photographs to decide that Lee, and not Johnny Beauchamp, had won.

Kyle Petty, Richard's only son, won the first race he ever entered at the Big D in an Automobile Racing Club of America event in 1979.

And it was at Daytona that Richard drove to his greatest victories, including his 200th, and supplied convincing credibility to his reign as king of the sport.

Whenever the few critics attempted to belittle his career accomplishments by claiming most of his victories and seven national championships were achieved in small events at out-of-the-way places, where there was not much competition, they could not deny the seven Daytona 500s that he won – all against the sport's best drivers.

For four decades, Daytona was something of a home away-from-home for the Pettys, but Richard told me during a 1981 interview that the only part of the city that he had any special feeling for was "that little plot over there they call Victory Lane."

By 1981, Daytona Beach had outgrown the laid-back atmosphere that Richard knew years earlier when only racers came to town to strut their stuff.

While still a friendly, enjoyable city that continued to open its arms to the racing crowd, Daytona was a mirror-image of what had happened to racing itself, especially during Speed Weeks in February. It grew bigger and bigger as the sport became more popular, and more than 100,000 people crammed into the area to pack motels, restaurants, and streets during Daytona 500 week.

"The place has changed tremendously," said Richard, who initially visited the city when Poppa Lee raced on the old beach course south of town.

"Used to be nobody was here but the racing crowd. I would race up and down the streets. They were deserted at night. If you wanted to check out your race car, you just worked it out on A-1-A. You couldn't do that today, of course."

He shrugged.

"Times change."

That they do, and it was difficult for me to believe when Richard drove his final Daytona 500 in 1992 that it had been eleven years since he had taken home a 500 trophy.

His seven Daytona 500 victories stretched between 1964 and 1981.

"A few of them I shouldn't have won, but I lost a few that I should have won. It all balances out," Richard told me.

There was no question about that first Daytona 500 victory in 1964. He drove a Plymouth powered by Chrysler's 426-cubic-inch engine and blew by everyone. "I'd always had a good handling car for the Daytona races, but that was the first time I had really good horsepower to go with it," Richard said.

Petty and other Chrysler drivers sat out the 1965 Daytona 500 because NASCAR outlawed Chrysler's powerful hemi engine. He came back with the hemi engine in 1966 to win the pole position and drove to a one-lap victory over Cale Yarborough in the race.

Richard won again in 1971, emerging triumphant in a down-to-the wire duel with A.J. Foyt and Buddy Baker. That gave him three Daytona 500 victories, and no one else had won more than one. Then, in 1973 and 1974, he became the first driver to put together consecutive victories in the event.

Richard had to wait five years before he won

his sixth Daytona 500, and he admitted it was one of those he should not have won. "I lucked into that one more than any race I ever won," he says.

Donnie Allison and Cale Yarborough were battling for the lead on the final lap when they wrecked on the backstretch. They then began a brawl in the third turn.

Richard, who had been too far behind to challenge either Allison or Yarborough, drove by the melee and barely beat Darrell Waltrip back to the finish line for the stunning victory.

Richard's victory came only a week after Kyle's career-opening ARCA victory, and Kyle congratulated his father by jumping on the hood of his car as he rolled down pit road on his way to Victory Lane.

During the post-race interview, Richard gave Kyle credit for teaching him the move that he made on Waltrip in the fourth turn that clinched the victory.

"I saw how Kyle drove low coming off the fourth turn last Sunday when he won the ARCA race, and I used that same move against Darrell," Richard said.

The third-turn brawl, which also included Donnie's older brother, Bobby, amused Richard as much as it did the national television audience. "As anxious as I was to get to Victory Lane, I was tempted to stop over there and watch them cats go at it," he said. "It reminded me of the old days. Back when Daddy was driving, that stuff happened all the time. You drove a bit and fought a bit. It was a matter of survival. You had to fight to protect yourself."

Richard's final Daytona 500 victory was not dumped into his lap, but it was almost as unexpected as his sixth.

Almost everyone agreed that Bobby Allison was the heavy favorite in 1981. He was driving a new Pontiac LeMans, which he put on the pole position. The car was the class of every other pre-race exercise, too.

Richard was irritated when I told him that Allison was saying the reason he had the fastest car was because of the hard work put into it by himself and crewmen.

"If that was the case, we would be out there setting a world-record speed," Richard replied. "You ask anyone on our team. We have worked as hard as anyone. If you measured the hours, everyone else would be way behind."

The trouble was the Petty crowd spent most of the winter working in the wrong direction.

Richard, who had traded his Dodge for a Chevrolet during the 1978 season, was itching to get back in a Dodge, and the new Mirada seemed just the car to relieve that itch.

It looked fast.

But it turned out just to look that way.

The car pushed too much air and struggled to get through the wind which prowls the long backstretch at Daytona. Richard knew he was in trouble with the Mirada when he tested and so much air got into the car that his driving goggles were almost blown away.

In desperation, and at a late hour, Petty parked the Dodge and bought a Buick. It was too late for him to conduct his own tests with the Buick, so he had to rely on advice from others to get the proper setup. This was not how Richard had won the previous six Daytona 500s, but he was brimming with confidence when he loaded the Buick for the trip to the Beach.

Richard continued to smile despite blowing a couple of engines during the week. He had told me once that he never started a Daytona 500 that he didn't think he was going to win, and that would be true this time, too.

He only laughed when I reminded him that everyone was predicting that Allison would run away from the the field for the victory.

"I am a hard-head," Richard said. "If Bobby has got me beat, he will have to prove it to me on Sunday. I have come here with the slowest car and won. I have come here with the fastest car and lost. And I've had the fastest car and won. You just can't tell what is going to happen because there is so much luck involved. We don't put as much effort as some do in getting the car fast for qualifying. But we do make it a point to have our car ready to run 500 miles when we come here."

The Allison Pontiac was as fast as advertised when the race began. It was a rabbit for everyone to chase, but Richard didn't seem the least bit interested in playing the role of the hound. He was content to run his own race, at his own pace.

Only the most loyal Petty fan was keeping an eye on the red and blue Buick, which was running at the tail end of the lead draft, when Allison's LeMans began to sputter. It had run out of fuel with about 25 miles remaining in the race and Allison had to coast down pit road for his final stop.

Ricky Rudd, Buddy Baker and Dale Earnhardt, who had been riding in Allison's draft, slowed quickly and followed Allison into the pits so they could make their final stops with the leader and remain in his draft. Each took on new tires and a full load of fuel.

When Richard did not play follow-the-leader and pit with the others, veteran Petty-watchers began looking at each other and trading smiles. They knew Richard had an ace up his sleeve that he was getting ready to play.

Richard had conferred with crew chief Dale Inman and brother Maurice by radio and they agreed that on his final pit stop he would pause only long enough for a splash of gasoline. Inman had done a tire check earlier and learned the Goodyears were showing little wear.

"I had a lot of faith in Dale," Richard said later. "If Dale had wanted to change all four tires, or send me out on three wheels, that was his decision."

Richard made his final stop a couple of laps after Allison and his followers. A roar went up from the crowd when it became apparent that Richard was going to get only a can of fuel, and no tires, which would give him a 10.7-second lead over Allison when he sped back onto the track.

He beat Allison to the checkered flag by eight seconds.

"Boys, we didn't have the fastest car, we just out-thunk them today," Richard said after taking Ol' 43 to Victory Lane.

It was a special moment, although none of us at the time recognized it as such.

Who could have believed that we had just witnessed Richard's final Daytona 500 triumph.

THE WAY IT WAS IN '67

Is Richard Petty the greatest stock car driver of all time? The record book certainly argues loudly that he is, but I am sure not everyone agrees.

Old timers tell me Curtis Turner had the most natural talent, and from the times I watched him race, I would not care to argue the point. I also have admired the skills of men such as David Pearson, Bobby Allison, Cale Yarborough, Dale Earnhardt, and Fireball Roberts.

Then, there was Lee Petty, Buck Baker, the Flock brothers, Darrell Waltrip, and LeeRoy Yarbrough.

The list goes on. You can make a good case for whomever you want.

But anyone who followed Richard Petty through the 1967 season, as I did, may have witnessed the greatest of them all in what certainly was the grandest season any driver ever experienced.

In 48 races that season, Richard won 27, finished second in seven others, and during one

In 48 races in the 1967 season, Richard won 27, finished second in seven others, and during one stretch rolled to 10 straight victories.

stretch rolled to 10 straight victories.

But it is not only the number of victories and records that Richard piled up during that joy-ride of a season that stands out in my memory. Just as impressive was how easily this country boy handled all of the fame and attention that came streaming down on his shoulders.

This was the year Richard became a legend; the year he was crowned "King Richard." And when we all understood we had never seen one of his kind before and were not likely to again.

I remember early in the season visiting with Richard before a Sunday afternoon race at Bristol International Raceway. He was sitting on the ground, a few feet away from his race car, leaning against a stack of tires. He stuck a piece of grass in his mouth and calmly watched as his brother, Maurice, and his cousin, Dale Inman, groomed the Number 43 Plymouth for another battle.

Pre-race butterflies?

None, whatsoever.

I have seen ducks more nervous about getting wet than Richard was about climbing into the race car. He sat there, laughing and telling jokes, as other drivers and mechanics walked over to join the conversation. It reminded me of my days growing up in a cotton mill village and watching workers talking and joking outside the fence before the whistle blew to call them into the factory.

Bill Taylor, a new NASCAR inspector, walked by the Petty Plymouth as Maurice cranked the engine.

"Looky there," mused Richard. "He is still new on the job. He has got to learn not to stand so close to the car while we are working it. He might see something that he shouldn't."

Richard kept a straight face until the others quit chuckling. Then he flashed a wide grin. "Naaaah," he said. "I don't mean that we would cheat. Heck, a man can't sleep at night if he wins a race that way."

He laughed.

"That is why I sleep twelve hours – a day," he said.

Someone suggested that Richard must have been sleeping days regularly after he won the Rebel 400 at Darlington Raceway the previous year. It had been an awesome performance by Ol' Blue.

"You know, I didn't know how bad I outran them boys until I looked at the films of the race and saw I just pulled away from everyone," Richard said. "I figured someone must have suspected something because when we got to Charlotte NASCAR had posted a sign that said the winning car would be checked from top to bottom after the race."

After another strong run in Ol' Blue was aborted by mechanical problems, Richard relieved Marvin Panch, driving another Petty Plymouth, and was co-driver in the victory, which was not reflected in the official record.

"Oh, there was nothing wrong with the car that Marvin was driving, so I didn't mind NASCAR looking at it as long as they wanted," Richard said. "But I bet there was a whole bunch of people who who would rather have looked under the hood of that Number 43 and didn't get the chance."

It was an old story, one that Petty told often, but it still drew laughs, and it was a way to help pass the time until the call to start engines.

Win or lose, Richard was just as calm and good-natured after races, too.

He already was the most popular driver on the circuit, just as his daddy had been before him, and there was no backlash to all the victories he was rolling up.

Richard was always around after races to sign autographs, to talk to the reporters and to chat with fans who came down from the stands or out of the infield to meet him.

After winning at Asheville, Petty propped himself on the pit wall, took off his black boots, and spent more than an hour signing autographs and talking.

One admirer stuck out his hand and asked Richard to sign it.

"Anything but checks," he said with a smile.

Indeed, during that magnificent season Petty did autograph everything but checks for his fans.

"You should have seen what some girl in Columbia asked me to sign," he told me with a wink. "Wow-eee! Did I like signing that autograph. Ever since, the guys on my crew hitch up the car as fast as they can and make it over to where I am signing autographs. They don't want to miss something like that again."

Richard seemed to genuinely enjoy the postrace sessions with the fans. It was a treat watching him work the crowds, and to the end of his career I never once saw him try to duck out on the fans after a victory.

I remember during the 1970s, after one victory at Talladega, a security officer escorted him out of the press box, where a large number of fans were waiting to get Richard's autograph.

After about a half-hour, the officer grabbed Petty's arm and said, "It's time to go."

Richard pulled back. "I don't know where you have to go, but I am going to stay right here and sign autographs for everyone who wants one," he said firmly.

An hour or so later, I looked out the press box door and saw Richard closing in on his last autograph. The security guard was gone.

Winston Cup races did not attract as many fans or as much media attention in 1967 as they did later on, but there always seemed to be reporters, cameramen, and fans constantly tugging for a piece of Richard.

He never complained and was never rude to anyone, which wasn't the case with some of the sport's newer stars in later years.

Whenever Richard did not completely hear a question, he always said "sir?"" or "ma'am?" in asking that it be repeated. It didn't matter if Richard was talking to a writer a few years younger than he, or to a Ford fan who was looking for a friendly argument.

"Saw you hit the wall a few times out there," said the large man wearing a smile and a Ford T-shirt.

"Yes, sir. I just do that to stay awake," Richard replied.

The only resentment toward Petty in 1967 came from a few drivers who, understandably, got tired of him winning so often. They grumbled that most of Richard's wins were on short tracks, where there was not much competition.

"That is why it feels so good to win these longer races," Richard said after a mid-summer victory at Bristol. "There are about seven or eight really good drivers I have to beat in the longer races."

For everyone else, though, there seemed to be only one driver and car to be concerned about beating – Richard and Ol' Blue.

Before the Bristol race, car owners Bud Moore and Junior Johnson looked long and hard at the Petty Plymouth, and Moore asked Johnson, "What are you going to do about Ol' Blue?"

Johnson replied that his driver that day, Darel Dieringer, was going to put a few laps on Richard.

Moore shook his head. "The only way for that to happen is for them to mess up in the pits or for Richard to have trouble on the track," he said.

Johnson nodded, and shrugged his huge shoulders. "I guess so. Anyone who puts a couple of laps on Ol' Blue has done a day's work."

In the race at Nashville, it didn't matter that Petty had trouble and dropped 14 laps down. He still came back to win the race.

Richard insisted throughout the season that his team was not doing anything differently than in previous years when his victory totals were fewer.

"We are getting smarter, but the others ought to be learning more, too," he reasoned. "Nothing has changed, and that is the truth."

Certainly, success did not spoil Richard, who still retained a good ol' boy's sense of humor and taste.

During the annual Northern Tour, which Petty enjoyed because he got to meet so many new fans, he and his team were treated to a New England clambake, which included a huge lobster.

It was a meal fit for a king, but not King Richard.

I had to laugh when Richard told me about it after he got back down South.

"You know, they boiled them lobster alive and those people up there really went after them," he said.

Richard tried a couple of bites, threw away the rest, and went to get some fried chicken.

DARLINGTON

Just as Richard Petty could not explain the reason he was so successful at Daytona, he never could pin-point why he had so few victories at Darlington International Raceway, the NASCAR circuit's oldest superspeedway.

I have never been able to figure that one out myself, and it has to be one of the biggest mysteries of his career.

The Darlington oval has frustrated more than one great driver, however, while others, such as David Pearson and Cale Yarborough, seemed to ride it as easily as backing out of their driveways.

Hall-of-Famer Bobby Isaac was one who never felt comfortable at Darlington. He used to tell me that he would rather take a beating than compete in the two races on the egg-shaped oval. "They ought to plow it up and turn it back into farmland," Isaac said often.

Darlington, with its narrow turns, built a reputation for punishing drivers and equipment. The apparent key to winning on the track was for a driver to take care of his equipment and drive a smooth, consistent pace.

Those were the same traits that made Richard the winningest driver in major racing history. But if he had depended on his record at Darlington, he might have gone broke.

Richard won only one Southern 500, two Rebel races, and had not been in Victory Lane at Darlington since 1967 as he entered his final year of racing.

All three of Richard's victories at Darlington came in 1966 and 1967 during a streak that gave no clue to the misfortune awaiting him at the track in years to come. In 1966, he won the Rebel 400 and finished second in the Southern 500. The following year he again won the Rebel and the Southern 500, becoming one of only a few drivers to sweep both events in the same season.

That was it. No more victories for the King on the Darlington track, which motorsports writer Benny Phillips named "The Lady in Black."

> Darlington, with its narrow turns, built a reputation for punishing drivers and equipment. The apparent key to winning on the track was for a driver to take care of his equipment and drive a smooth, consistent pace.

Richard told me he did not know how to explain his lack of success at Darlington. "It just doesn't make sense. How can anyone explain why I can win so many races at other tracks, and come here and race against the same people and not win any more than I have?"

He speculated that part of the problem might have been that he was not in top physical condition for several of the events. He could remember five or six times getting hurt right before the Darlington races. "The Bristol race comes right before the Southern 500 and I have crashed there three or four times. Once I cracked some ribs in a race at Asheville before I came here."

Richard agreed with me that his driving style seemed well-suited for the Darlington track. "It really should be a great place for me," he said, nodding his head. "The only way I can see it is that our luck has been really bad at Darlington. What makes it even stranger is that my car ran well at the track from the first time I went there. I guess it is just that the Pettys weren't supposed to win that much at Darlington.

"Of all the tracks that we run, luck is more of a factor at Darlington than any other. I remember a race that Cale Yarborough won. He was

Richard holds the trophy during a rare visit to Darlington Raceway's victory circle after a 1967 victory.

involved in a wreck that eliminated a couple of other top contenders near the end of the race. Cale spun out, too, but he was the only one of the leaders who could get back in the race. If that is not luck, I don't know what is."

Richard, though, did have the pleasure of winning the historic 55th race of his career on the Darlington course in the 1967 Rebel. That allowed him to become NASCAR's winningest driver, moving him one victory ahead of his father, Lee, who had held the record.

Richard drove a Plymouth Belvedere to a one-lap victory over David Pearson, who was making his debut as driver of the Holman-Moody Ford. Richard dominated the event by leading 266 of 291 laps, and the victory snapped a five-race winning streak by Fords on the super-speedways.

Lee Petty watched from a tower near pit road as his son replaced him in the record books. "I was pulling for him all the way," he said. "It couldn't happen to a nicer guy."

Richard, then 29 years old, was glad he was able to break his father's record by winning at a major speedway. As funny as it might seem now, Richard also commented that he hoped he could win another 55 races before he ended his career.

He was able to do that in only the next three years, but just one of the victories was at Darlington, where no other Petty had ever won either.

When Richard's son, Kyle, began his career by driving a limited schedule in 1978, he asked his father for permission to enter the Southern 500 and was told to wait until he got more experience.

Richard informed Kyle that the only thing he could enter at Darlington was the golf tournament held during race week.

"He asked me why," Richard said, "and I told him that I didn't know if I was ready to run at that place, and I knew dang well that he wasn't."

MOVIES, RECORDS AND COMICS

Long before Tom Cruise jumped into a stock car to speed across the big screen as the star of the 1991 movie, "Days of Thunder," Richard Petty already had brought NASCAR racing to the nation's theaters.

The year was 1972, and I guess that was the moment I fully understood just how big a superstar Richard had become.

I mean, everyone who was around Richard during his rocket-ride to the top knew he was something special, and I never underestimated his talents or popularity.

But this was during a period of time that NASCAR racing was still trying to outgrow its Southern roots and establish itself as a national sport. Races were not on television every weekend, and the only event that attracted much national attention was the Daytona 500.

But Richard became bigger than the sport in my eyes the day he told me he was going to play himself in a movie about the family racing team.

It wasn't one of those low-budget, back-room productions either.

Richard thought having a comic book about him was more special than the movie or the record, and he got a big laugh out of the comic book the first time he read it.

Richard shared star billing with Darren McGavin, a fine character actor who did a great job of portraying Lee Petty. The script was written by Ed Lasko, a regular writer for the popular television series Mission: Impossible.

This was big-time stuff.

"The cat who edited the movie also did The Godfather," Richard said.

I just could not understand why Richard was having to play himself, unless John Wayne was not available.

Richard explained it all by saying the producer told him, "No one could play me but me, and I had to agree with him."

After seeing the movie, I had to agree with both of them. It just would not have been the same seeing anyone else crawling into Number 43 and pretending to be the King.

Richard did a good job, considering he didn't have any acting experience or lessons. But he didn't much care for acting and never considered it as a second career.

"There is too much running around and waiting," he said. "I enjoyed it for a couple of weeks, but I wouldn't want to do it all the time."

Richard didn't think what he did was acting, either. That was because he was playing himself.

"All I had to do was read the lines," he explained. "They couldn't tell me what kind of facial expressions to make. I was the only one who knew how Richard Petty would react to an incident."

Richard was pleased the movie was not strictly a racing flick. "It is more of a family picture, something that appeals to more than just the racing crowd," he said.

The movie was released under the title: The Petty Story: No. 43. It didn't win any Oscars, but I don't remember it receiving any bad reviews either. It was still being played on late-night television and was in some video rental shops two decades later when Richard prepared to end his driving career.

The Petty story was told in another unusual way in 1980 when Richard starred in his own comic book.

The comic book began with Richard defeating Darrell Waltrip for the 1979 championship, then skipped back through the years to 1928 when 16-year-old Lee Petty traded his bicycle for a beat-up Model T Ford.

Like the movie, it was well done, as were most of the things in which Richard was involved.

The script was written by STP publicist Harvey Duck, a former Chicago sports writer. The drawings were by Bob Kane, who created the comic book hero Batman.

Richard, who read the Batman and Robin funny books when he was a boy, admitted he was honored to find himself a comic book hero. "And it is another first for me," he reminded. "I was the first driver to have a movie made about him, and now I am the first in racing to be in a comic book."

Richard also joined a group of other drivers in the 1970s to record a country music album. He sang Roger Miller's song, King of the Road, of course.

But Richard thought having a comic book about him was more special than the movie or the record. "Most books like that are classics, and not many of them are about living people," he said.

Richard got a big laugh out of the comic book the first time he read it. "I didn't go through it to be critical, but to just enjoy it," he said.

The comic related how Richard, brother Maurice, and cousin Dale Inman raced against each other as youngsters, first in wagons and then on bicycles. Miffed that Richard was winning all the races, Dale and Maurice built a water hole on the race course.

Richard was the first to reach the puddle. When he tried to go through it, he spun out in the mud, much to the delight of Dale and Maurice, who were watching from a safe distance.

Richard said the stories in the book were based on actual happenings.

I told Richard that about the only thing left for him to do was to get his own television series. Something like "Car 43, Where Are You," or "Leave It to Richard."

"I wouldn't have time for that," he said. "I'm

satisfied with just being in a funny book. But I guess some of them other cats are right when they say the Pettys are a pretty funny family."

Richard wasn't interested in making another movie, either. "I did two in one when I made it — my first and my last," he said.

But he did act again, this time giving a live stage performance.

It was when former Petty rival Fred Lorenzen was inducted into racing's Hall of Fame in Darlington in 1979. Part of the program was a play, presented by members of the High Point, N.C., Shakespeare Festival Group, about Lorenzen's racing career.

As was the case in the movie, no one could play Richard but himself.

That he did. Again.

THE OTHER CATS

At the peak of his career, Richard Petty became the standard by which all other stock car racers were measured. If a driver had a great season, it was great because he won more races that year than Richard. But a driver who had a great career had to measure it in some other way, because in that department no one was ever going to beat him. It is unlikely, if not impossible, for anybody ever to win more races than Richard Petty.

For two decades, the '60s and '70s, Richard was the target for other top teams and drivers, and it was only natural that he would be involved in every major rivalry that developed during those years. That gave him immense satisfaction.

"It was always me against whoever else was winning at the time," Richard said. "For a year or two it might be me against this cat, and then the next two or three years me against some other cat. I was always a part of it."

One of the most interesting sessions I had with Richard was in 1978 when he agreed to

For two decades, the '60s and '70s, Richard was the target for other teams and drivers, and it was only natural that he would be involved in every major rivalry that developed during those years.

evaluate the drivers he had competed against during the first two decades of his career. As usual, he was candid as he went down the list. He did not rank the drivers as being the best or worst, but commented on how he saw them as fellow competitors.

Not surprisingly, the first driver Richard mentioned was David Pearson, with whom he had many memorable duels.

"Pearson will try to figure out in advance what is going on in a race and what is liable to happen," Richard said. "His biggest asset, along with having all of that talent, is patience. He is calm and collected. He is not nearly as hard on equipment as most of the others."

Cale Yarborough, who won three straight titles during the '70s while driving for Junior Johnson, had a style much different. "Cale is just a hard driver," Richard said. "He will run wide open all the time. He only gives up when he gets way behind, and that doesn't happen very often. He depends a lot on his reflexes. He will drive into a situation first and then try to work his way out of it."

Ironically, although Richard won five championships and Cale three during the '70s, they seldom were locked together in a head-to-head rivalry on the track.

"It was just one of them deals that he would outrun me or I would outrun him. I don't remember finishing second to Cale, or him finishing second to me that many times. We had our careers that ran parallel for several years, but I didn't cross paths with him as much as with some of the others."

Richard thought Darrell Waltrip, in his early years, had a style of driving that resembled Cale's. "He gets into a situation and then tries to figure how to get out of it," Richard said. "But Darrell is a good driver, and he is going to be super if he continues to improve. I wouldn't do some of the things that he does, but he seems able to get by with a lot of them."

Later in his career, Waltrip developed a more patient style, similar to that of Richard and Pearson.

Richard thought the "money driver" in the '70s was Benny Parsons. "When everything is working good, Benny is hard to beat. If I was going to hire someone to go out and drive for me to make money, Benny would be my first choice," Richard said. "He doesn't take many chances, and people who don't know him personally would not believe how easy-going he is. He drives like that, too, and sometimes he doesn't push as hard as he should. He doesn't want to mess up anybody, and he ought to be more aggressive.

"But the thing I like about Benny is he is rarely ever in trouble. If the car isn't handling right, he will back off and keep it under control. Some of the others try to stay out front and push it until they get in trouble."

Richard thought Bobby Allison "is as good of driver as I ever ran against when everything is going right for him." He didn't think much of Allison the times he tried to run his own team.

"Bobby runs best when he drives for someone else, like when he was with Junior Johnson or Holman-Moody and didn't have to be concerned with keeping up his own car. The way racing has become, it is hard for anyone to do that."

Donnie Allison, Bobby's younger brother, also had an up-and-down career and never developed a memorable rivalry with Richard. "For some reason or other, every time Donnie would get in a decent car, something would happen and he would be out of a ride again," Richard said. "But give him good equipment, and he runs well."

Buddy Baker was Richard's choice for being the unluckiest driver he had competed against. "Buddy is better than his record shows, and he should have won more races than he has," Richard said. "He can be out front leading a race, and something just falls off his car. But when he has good equipment, no one runs any harder than Buddy."

Drivers during the 1960s who impressed Richard, other than his father, included Junior Johnson, Curtis Turner, Fireball Roberts, Tim Flock and Fred Lorenzen – Richard's first major rival.

"Junior was one heck of a driver," Richard said. "Curtis was a real good dirt-track racer, and Fireball was at his best on asphalt."

About his father, Richard said, "Well, he had to be fairly decent to accomplish all he did. He handled everything, even towing the race car to the tracks, and when he quit he had won more races than anyone else up to that time."

Richard's rivalry with Lorenzen was a natural.

"I was driving a Plymouth and Freddie was driving a Ford, and that automatically put us against each other as far as most fans were concerned. We were both doing pretty good, and were about the same age, and that was during a period when you had Fireball, Daddy, Curtis, and Junior as the established stars. They were from the old school, and here comes a couple of younger people running up front and running good and that sorta caught the fancy of the spectators a little more, you know.

"Freddie would run good and I would run good. Even if we both ran bad, it seemed we were still racing against each other. There for four or five years it was Lorenzen against Petty, Petty against Lorenzen. He was super good and real smart. But, really, he quit when he was still young and didn't stay around that long."

"Fearless Freddie," as Lorenzen, was known, retired from the Holman-Moody ride in 1967. A few years later, he attempted a couple of comebacks and when they were not successful he returned permanently to his home in Illinois, where he became a wealthy real estate broker.

Lorenzen always said Richard was the toughest opposition he had during his career. "Richard was a lot like me. He raced with his brains. I worried more about him than anyone else because I knew he was likely to finish the race. Drivers like Junior Johnson ran strong for a while, but they were not there at the end too much. You always knew Richard was going to be there to race you at the end."

Lorenzen also respected the men behind Richard, Dale Inman and Maurice Petty. "Dale was the sly fox. He could always figure me out, and what my team was doing," Freddie said. "They were a tough bunch to beat."

The Early Years

Brothers Richard and Maurice take a break before a round of qualifying.

The Early Years

Richard goes to work in his "office" during his record-breaking 1967 season.

The Early Years

During the 1967 season, Richard won a record-setting 27 races, including 10 in a row during one stretch.

The Early Years

Richard finishes a close second to David Pearson, but ahead of Bobby Allison, in the 1972 Firecracker 400 at Daytona International Speedway.

The Early Years

After winning his inaugural race under STP sponsorship in 1973, Richard is greeted by then-STP boss Andy Granatelli and his wife, Dolly.

Not everyone liked the Fu Manchu mustache Richard grew for the 1973 Daytona 500.

The Early Years

Richard chases rival
David Pearson during the
1974 Firecracker 400.
Pearson won the race, and
Petty finished second.

The Early Years

The crash of 1976: Richard and David Pearson crashed on the last lap of the 1976 Daytona 500. Pearson barely made it to the finish line for the victory.

The Early Years

Major rivals Bobby Allison and Richard Petty used their publicized rivalry to attract a sponsorship deal.

RICHARD AND BOBBY

Bobby Allison is among my favorite all-time drivers, and without question one of the fiercest competitors ever to race the NASCAR circuit.

He worked his way from the bottom to the top during a fabulous driving career that ended in 1988 with a horrendous crash at Pocono Raceway. He was fortunate to survive.

Through most of Bobby's early years on the circuit, after he became a winner, he seemed to have a chip on his shoulder when it came to racing against Richard. Maybe that was to be expected because of the differences in their backgrounds.

Richard used to become irritated if anyone even hinted that he just stepped into a winning operation and made the most of it. "No one every gave the Pettys nothing," he reminded. "We worked for everything we got."

They did, of course, and worked very hard.

But Richard was fortunate to begin his career at the highest level. In only a few years he was winning races regularly and establishing his rep-

> **B**obby Allison's nature was to be super-competitive, and he was determined to be the best driver on the circuit. To do that he knew he had to knock King Richard off his throne.

utation as a superstar – and working every mile of the way.

Allison started out at the very bottom. He spent his early years on NASCAR's minor league circuits, where he became a regular winner and a national champion before getting a self-made opportunity to compete in racing's spotlight.

Once on NASCAR's elite circuit, Allison complained frequently that the reporters who covered NASCAR, who during the late '60s were based almost entirely in the Carolinas and Virginia, were biased in behalf of Richard and unwilling to give him the credit he deserved. Allison based his race team in Alabama.

Bobby's nature was to be super-competitive, and he was determined to be the best driver on the circuit. To do that he knew that he had to knock King Richard off his throne.

Richard, of course, was just as determined not to yield, and I anticipated that the Allison-Petty rivalry eventually would explode with the built-up fury of a volcano.

Richard told me it was the only rivalry he had during his career that boiled over beyond the race track and became a conflict of personalities. "All the others were just a part of racing, and when the races were over that was it," Richard said. "But the rivalry with Bobby got to be one of those slam-bang deals, and from time to time the media tried to make more out of it than it was. I think both of us started taking it personally, too."

Allison says the feud began during his second full season on the top NASCAR circuit. Richard was trying to make a pass and Allison refused to back off or give him room to do it quick enough.

"I was going to let Richard get around me, but he tried to go ahead sooner than I wanted," Bobby said. "We hit and he bent his fender and had to pit. That cost him the victory, and I knew he was mad, because I would have been, too, if it had happened to me. After the race, Richard's brother, Maurice, slugged me."

The feud flickered to life again in 1971 at Talladega while Bobby was driving for Holman-Moody, and again the next year when Bobby was behind the wheel of Junior Johnson's race car. "I never felt Richard was afraid I would steal his thunder, but I could be wrong," Bobby told me when I asked about that.

"I know Richard had gotten real use to winning, and then it was Richard against Bobby, and a whole lot of times when I won, he would finish second. But, out of all the fender-banging that went on between us, I would say less than one percent was intentional. We both were giving 150 percent effort and not yielding an inch or backing off. Our driving styles were different, too, in the way we worked the accelerator and brakes. That caused some of the banging in the turns, and it would get the press and fans excited."

Richard said driving styles were not the only difference. "I wouldn't say Bobby was more competitive than some of my other rivals, but he wasn't quite as laid-back. Even though most of the others had grown up on the short tracks, they had been away from it for awhile. Bobby came in and he had won some modified championships on the short tracks and I always felt he felt I was the one to beat, the one he was aiming at. He was good enough to run with me, and I was good enough to run with him.

"It just so happened that he had a super good car and I did, too, and for five or six races we came right to the flag racing each other for the victory. Then it got to be more than just racing each other. We got to beating on each other."

In the separate interviews I had with them over the years, Bobby and Richard generally agreed about how they were able to settle their differences.

"We finally just went face-to-face and said, 'Hey, guys, we got to call a halt to this thing,' and that is what we did," Richard said.

The truce talks took place behind a truck in the garage area. "It had started getting too deep and the time had come for both of us to back up a little," Bobby said.

A few years later, when Bobby was in one of his down cycles, the memory of those bitter clashes between two great drivers came rushing back following an incident at North Wilkesboro Speedway. This was in 1977. Richard held a half-lap lead and was trying to stretch it even more when he moved up on Allison and prepared to put him another lap down.

Allison held his line against the leader, and when Richard attempted to drive around, Allison's car slipped in the turn and Richard instinctively jerked the steering wheel. His red and blue Dodge drifted toward the top of the track, slid on little bits of loose asphalt, and went into a spin that cost him the victory.

There was speculation that the incident might re-ignite the feud between the two drivers.

It didn't.

I talked to Bobby the next week at Charlotte and learned their truce was still strong.

"I haven't said anything to Richard about what happened in Wilkesboro," he told me. "If he was mad about what happened, there would not have been any use in talking to him. If he wasn't mad, he knew that I didn't mean for that to happen."

Bobby had talked to Maurice, however. "I told him that I was sorry it happened, because I knew Richard had not won on the short tracks in two years. I could understand his frustration. I haven't won a Winston Cup race on any kind of track in two years."

Allison smiled and nodded his head when I recalled the fender-banging duels he and Richard once had.

"I will tell you something about those duels," Bobby told me that day. "They got to be pretty bitter, but there is a special comradeship among the drivers on this circuit that you won't find in any other sport. In most professional sports you have hundreds or thousands of competitors.

There is only a handful running up front on this circuit, and I guess that makes us closer.

"Richard and I would have a bitter race at one track, but at the next race if there was anything I needed, I didn't mind walking up to him and asking if he would loan it to me. If he had it, he would give it to me, and I would do the same thing for him. But once the race began, we were back at it again."

I asked Richard then if he and Allison might ever be friends. "Right now, I am not good friends with any driver because I have to race against them, and try to beat them," he said. "But Bobby and I learned to respect each other, and that is the big thing. At one time I think we had lost that respect."

Richard paused for a moment, removed his cigar, and smiled. "But, yeah. I think when we are through racing each other that we can be friends," he said.

When I told Bobby what Richard had said, he nodded his head.

"That is pretty neat," he said.

And when they were through racing each other, finished by that terrible accident that took Bobby from behind the wheel, that is exactly what happened. They became friends.

RICHARD AND DAVID

I suppose everyone has his favorite era in NASCAR Winston Cup racing. For some it might have been the "traveling circus" days, when NASCAR teams roamed the country and raced at every available dust bowl. For others it might have been the 1980s, when the sport's popularity began sweeping the nation and just about every race could be watched on television.

For me, the golden era was during the '70s.

Richard Petty was in this lane, David Pearson in the other. They rode the towering banks of the superspeedways high, wide, and handsome, battling each other fender-to-fender and bumper-to-bumper in the championship groove.

Stock car racing's most memorable rivalry began on a hot August night in 1963 on the flat, dirt track at Columbia, S.C. David was 28 years old and a graduate of Whitney Mill village in Spartanburg, S.C. Richard was two years younger and a graduate of the Petty School of Racing in Level Cross, N.C.

Richard Petty won 200 races and in 30 of them David Pearson was second. Pearson won 105 races, and in 33 of them Petty was second.

Richard drove a Plymouth to victory by a nine-second margin over runner-up Pearson, who was wheeling a Dodge built by Cotton Owens. It was the twenty-fifth career victory for Richard, who was in only his fifth compete season on the circuit. Pearson had won only three races, all coming in 1961, his rookie year.

None of us who saw that race in 1963 had any idea we were witnessing the beginning of a rivalry between two drivers who would become the winningest in stock car racing history, the only two to win more than 100 races.

Richard won 200 races and in 30 of them Pearson ran second. Pearson won 105 and in 33 of them Richard was second.

"During my full career, the rivalry with David was bigger than any of the others," Richard says. "It was a good rivalry because it never got personal. It was all on the race track. And, considering how many times each of us finished second to the other, we knocked each other out of a lot of victories over the years."

The rivalry took off after Pearson left Owens' stable of Dodges and replaced Fred Lorenzen, who retired from the Holman-Moody Ford ride in 1967. Pearson finished second to Richard at Darlington in his first start for his new Ford team.

But it was not until Pearson joined the Wood Brothers' Mercury team in 1972 that the rivalry really began flying and captured the interest of race fans everywhere. "David had a lot of fans, and I had a lot of fans, and we both were running up front. That is what made the rivalry," Richard explained when I asked how it developed.

In the minds of many, including myself, the most dramatic and spectacular finish in auto racing history involved Richard and David in the 1976 Daytona 500 as they battled through the final lap for the checkered flag. A collision off the fourth turn wrecked both cars, but Pearson was able to keep his engine running and crept across the finish line at about 20 miles per hour for the victory.

It was not the most controversial finish between the two superstars – just the most spectacular. There had been a couple of spats, one minor and one major, that preceded the Big Crash.

In the 1972 Firecracker 400 at Daytona International Speedway, David engaged Richard in a mild controversy after beating him to the finish line by only five feet. After crawling out of his car in the garage, Richard told reporters that he knew Pearson had him beat on the last lap and his strategy was to hold off Bobby Allison for second place, which he did.

Pearson laughed when he heard what Richard was saying. He thought Richard had goofed and was not willing to admit it.

"I usually know what to expect from Richard, because he is about the best driver on the circuit, and I have been racing against him for about thirteen years," Pearson said.

"He just goofed today. He should have tried to pass me on the backstretch instead of waiting to make his move in the fourth turn. Richard's car was the fastest one in the race, but even a slower car can use the slingshot to pass on the backstretch. When he didn't do that, and I got to the third turn, I knew there was no way he could get around me then."

Richard was content to stick by his explanation, and I don't remember much more being said about the incident after the teams loaded up their cars and pulled out of the speedway.

In the same race the following year, though, a major controversy exploded between the two after Pearson won again. It is the only time I ever witnessed Richard losing his cool, and the only time racing's two greatest winners showed public anger with each other.

Pearson, nicknamed the "Silver Fox," because of his slyness, was in the lead entering the final lap of the race. He had slowed down a lap or two earlier, hoping Richard would take the point and give him the chance to use the slingshot to pass on the backstretch on the final lap.

Richard didn't take the bait, so Pearson faked a blown engine just beyond the flag stand at the beginning of the final lap. With Richard in a tight draft with him, Pearson's No. 21 Mercury slowed dramatically and he eased it toward the bottom of the track.

After Richard drove by the Mercury, Pearson brought his car back to full speed. He sprung the slingshot on the backstretch and whizzed by Richard for the victory.

Richard was furious, and when we invited him to the press box to tell his side of the story, he accepted.

I had never seen Richard as angry as he was that day, and I don't know if it was because Pearson had out-foxed him or because he thought Pearson's trick really was as unsafe as he contended.

"It was a dumb thing for Pearson to do," Richard told the writers who gathered around him in the press box. "He could have wrecked both of us. It is just not like David to pull a trick like that and not let the other driver know what is happening. Usually, when you blow an engine or slow down like that, you raise your hand so the driver behind you knows to back off. David didn't do anything."

Richard said he did not have time to know what was happening when Pearson's car slowed. He had to hit the brakes and make a real sharp turn to the right to keep from slamming into the rear of Pearson's car.

"After I got out front of him by about 300 feet and then saw him coming at me, I figured it out," Richard said.

It did not take long for David and Richard to begin arguing between themselves. Things got real hot when Pearson told Richard that maybe he should get the Wood Brothers to build him a race car. Richard's face glowed with anger, and he bit tightly into the cigar between his teeth.

A few second later, staring directly at Pearson, Richard said again that Pearson usually drove much saner than he had on the final lap of the Firecracker. The two argued about who had the faster car, and who could have passed who where. Finally, Pearson laughed and shook his head in disgust.

"You see who is getting red in the face," Richard said as he nodded toward David.

Pearson replied that his move had not been dangerous. "If he had run in the back of me, it wouldn't have done anything but knocked me forwards," David said.

It was Richard's turn to laugh sarcastically and shake his head in disgust before walking out of the press box.

The blistering confrontation was a big story for the next several days, although both drivers had nothing more to say about the other after leaving the track.

If anyone expected the feud to erupt again in the next big race at Atlanta, however, they were mistaken. Richard even joked about it after he won with Pearson finishing second this time.

As Richard entered the Atlanta press box, he cut his eyes over his shoulders, looked real nervous, and asked, "Where's David?"

Richard insisted here was no grudge to settle with Pearson. "I beat David at Michigan the week before Daytona. He beat me there, and I beat him here."

Richard had told me several times there was not another driver on the circuit he respected more than Pearson. Nothing had changed.

"I learned something at Daytona that I did not know about David. But I would still rather follow him around a race track than anyone else.

If he should go through a fence and I was right behind him, I would follow him, because I would figure he knew what he was doing," Richard said.

Neither Richard nor David leveled any angry charges at the other after the Big Crash in the 1976 Daytona 500. Richard did, however, break the promise he made in 1973 to never again go to the press box unless he was the winner.

We wanted to hear Richard's side of the story, and after repeated requests he finally agreed to join Pearson in the press box.

Richard had been in the lead at the beginning of the last lap. David took the point on the backstretch. Richard went low, looking to regain the lead off the third turn, but his Dodge shot up the track and tapped Pearson's Mercury.

Richard kept his Dodge low as the two cars came off the fourth turn, and he seemed to regain the lead momentarily. Suddenly, the red and blue Dodge slipped up into Pearson's lane, sending it into the outside wall. The Mercury bounced off the wall and spun down the track, across the infield, and struck another car on pit road, which seemed to point it back toward the race track.

Richard's car spun wildly down the speedway, apparently headed for the finish line. It stalled some twenty-five feet short of reaching it. He tried to restart his engine and some crewmen raced to give him a push until they saw Pearson's beat-up machine barely rolling under the checkered flag.

Wanting to avoid any confrontation between the two crews, who had no idea what had happened to cause the wreck, Richard ran from his disabled car over to David's after it had taken the checkered flag. Richard accepted blame for the accident.

However, after watching replays of the video tape in the press box, Richard was not as sure that he was responsible. He could see that he hit Pearson between the third and fourth turns and apologized for that.

"But I am not apologizing for the final wreck," Richard said.

Richard seemed in good spirits and still feeling hyper from all the excitement as he wiped his face with a towel and told his version of what happened.

"When my car got sideways, I hit the brakes. I just wanted to get the car back under control. I didn't give a dern if I ever got to the finish line at that point."

A few weeks earlier Richard had spent ten days in the hospital for treatment of an ulcer. "Now, I've probably got two ulcers to worry about," he moaned.

Pearson, of course, was in good spirits, too.

Although he had won three Firecracker 400 races at the Big D, this was his first Daytona 500 triumph. He disagreed with Richard about who was responsible for the final bump that led to the Big Crash, but he was not going to argue.

Who was responsible?

I have watched replays of the wreck many times. The only thing I can see is that two great drivers – the two greatest of all time, in my book – came charging off the fourth turn high, wide, and handsome, riding the championship groove, and neither was willing to back off and finish second.

It was just racin' at its finest, I guess.

Buddy Baker, below, joined the Petty racing team for the 1971 and 1972 seasons. At right, the twin STP-Dodge racing cars, with Richard in front, are caught in a flying shot at Talladega, and that's how they finished in the 1971 Daytona 500.

PETTY SCHOOL OF RACING

Everyone knows that Lee Petty began Petty Enterprises, winning races and championships before retiring and leaving the driving to his eldest son, Richard. Most people know, too, that Richard's brother, Maurice, drove a few races in the early '60s before concentrating on the mechanical end of the business, and that Richard's son, Kyle, also began his driving career with the family team.

What everyone may not know, however, is that a lot of people whose last name was not Petty drove for Petty Enterprises.

The list reads like a Who's Who in racing: Bobby Myers, Tiny Lund, Jim Reed, Johnny Beauchamp, Bobby Johns, Jim Paschal, Marvin Panch, Bob Welborn, Dan Gurney, Hershel McGriff, LeeRoy Yarbrough, Buck Baker, Joe Weatherly, Jim Hurtubise, Pete Hamilton, Buddy Baker, Dick Brooks, and Morgan Shepherd.

Some drove in only one or two events in a Petty Enterprises car, but several were regulars who drove in a team with Lee or Richard. From 1957 until 1974, it was not unusual for Petty

A lot of people whose last name was not Petty drove for Petty Enterprises. The list reads like a Who's Who of racing.

Enterprises to field more than one car per race. A couple of years Petty Enterprises entered three cars in 10 or more races.

One of the most successful of those team drivers was Hall-of-Famer Jim Paschal, whose trademarks were a short haircut, a cigar, and a driving style as smooth as his quiet, non-assuming personality. He won nine races for Petty Enterprises during the early '60s.

When Paschal was inducted into the Hall-of-Fame in 1977, Richard told me that during the early years of his career he had learned more about racing from Paschal than anyone except his father.

"Jim was ten years ahead of his time by being a smart driver," Richard said. "He didn't break equipment, and he was usually in the thick of things at the end of the race."

In later years, others passed through Petty Enterprises looking to learn from Richard, and hoping to make the most of the opportunity to drive a Petty car.

Buddy Baker could not have been more

delighted to drive a Dodge out of the Petty stable during the 1971 season. He and Richard, still in a Plymouth, were the only factory drivers on the circuit that year.

A few days before the 1971 Daytona 500, I asked Baker if he had been around the Pettys long enough to understand why they had been so successful. He smiled and nodded his head.

"The Pettys don't have any life other than racing," Buddy told me. "After practice at the tracks, the whole crew goes back to the motel and sits around talking about what they can do the next day to go faster.

"When they are home, everyone lives right around the garage. They wake up, walk across Lee's putting green to the garage, stop only for lunch, and work until night. They go to bed, get up the next morning, and do it all over again."

Buddy, whose reputation was that of a hard-driving but excitable charger, figured just being associated with Richard had made him a better driver.

"Richard is something else. I have never seen anyone who can stay as calm and easy-going as he does. Nothing ever bothers him. He can be in a restaurant and the waitress might spill hot coffee on him and it wouldn't bother him a bit. I wish I could be more like that."

Another thing that impressed Baker was Richard's mechanical knowledge. He knew the mechanics of a race car as well as any of the crewmen. "When he's at the garage, he stays under the car, working on it," Buddy said.

Richard and Buddy were the class of the 1971 Daytona 500, and they began the event with the understanding that neither would endanger the other's chances for winning. If it came to a shoot-out, the driver whose car was clocked the slowest would back off and let the other go.

Thus, with about twenty laps remaining, Richard thought the victory was in his pocket, barring any unusual circumstances. His crew had clocked both cars, and Richard's was faster by about a half-second per lap. Both drivers were flashed messages that signaled Richard was to stay in front and Baker was not to race him for the victory.

Richard saw the message. Buddy was too busy racing to notice the one from his crew. It didn't matter, however, as Buddy experienced a handling problem with his Dodge during the final laps and backed off on his own, allowing Richard a smooth drive to the checkered flag.

It was Richard's third Daytona 500 victory and he was delighted that Petty cars swept the front two positions. "This is a heckuva accomplishment for Petty Enterprises," Richard declared.

Although it was Richard's first Daytona 500 victory since 1966, it was the second straight in racing's most prestigious event for Petty Enterprises. The year before, Richard had an early mechanical problem and watched young teammate Pete Hamilton win in a down-to-the-wire duel with veteran David Pearson.

Hamilton, a handsome blond-haired, blue-eyed Yankee from Dedham, Mass., was said to be hand-picked by Richard to be his teammate, and he quickly proved that Richard was an excellent judge of racing talent.

"I have always admired Richard, and I asked him a while back about driving a Petty team car,"

Hamilton explained when asked how he had gotten the ride. "One day he called me and said 'Come on up to Randleman. I think I have a job for you.'"

Hamilton had been rookie-of-the-year on the top NASCAR circuit in 1968. He failed to win because of not having good equipment, and in 1969 he drove on the Grand American circuit, where he was the winningest driver. Then came the call from Richard that put him in a Petty Plymouth for fifteen races in 1970.

"There is a lot for me to learn from Richard, but I feel there are still a few victories left in this car," Hamilton said following his Daytona 500 triumph. He was right, too.

Hamilton swept both races that year on the superfast track at Talladega, Ala., but at the end of the season he found himself squeezed out of the Petty ride because of factory cutbacks. There was only one factory Plymouth on the circuit in 1971, and it had Richard's name on it.

After winning three superspeedway races with the Pettys, Hamilton never won another Winston Cup race. He soon disappeared from the circuit after spending the 1971 season in Cotton Owens' Dodge. The two argued constantly. Owens said it was because Hamilton couldn't get used to driving for someone other than the Pettys.

"Pete had been with the Pettys, and he wanted to do everything the way they had done them," Owens told me. "I know the Pettys have a great team. But just as you can't copy someone else's writing style, I couldn't copy the way someone else built race cars. Pete figured he couldn't learn anything from me."

The Pettys were not the only ones who could build winning race cars, but during the golden years in the '60s and '70s there was not a better place for a young, inexperienced mechanic to get an education.

Just like the long list of great drivers who drove for Petty Enterprises through the years, a large crowd of excellent mechanics either began or furthered their careers at what some respectfully call "Petty University." A few of them were Jake Elder, Red Myler, Tim Petty, Ken Wilson, Robin Pemberton and Barry Dodson.

I talked to Dodson about his experience at Petty Enterprises in 1989, the year he was crew chief for Winston Cup champion Rusty Wallace. Barry was a crewman for Richard between 1972 and 1977.

"If anybody could pick a place in those days that he wanted to work, and where he could get an education about race cars, Petty Enterprises was the place," Barry said. "I started out doing body work. That was all I knew how to do, really. The Pettys taught me how to build cars."

Richard also taught Dodson what it took to be a winner.

"The best lesson I learned the whole time I was there was to do things the right way and not to take any short cuts. It is something that I practiced throughout my career. Richard would tell me to do things this way or that way, and if I messed up he would make me change it."

Barry recalled a race at Talladega, when Richard drove into the pits with a cracked windshield. Barry quickly crawled through the right-side window to tape the windshield from inside the car. He rushed to apply the tape as quickly as possible in hopes of getting Richard back on the track without losing a lap. In his haste, Barry barely wrinkled the tape as he pressed it against the windshield.

"Richard yelled for me to remove the wrinkled tape, and put it on smooth," Barry said. "He didn't seem angry or upset, and during the whole time was just as calm as he could be. He just wanted the job done right. When I got the tape on, the way he wanted, he looked over and said, 'Now, that's better.'"

That is one of my favorite Richard Petty stories, because it says so much about the way the man is, and why he was so successful. No matter if it cost him the chance of winning, Richard stubbornly taught a young mechanic a valuable lesson that day.

There would be other races he won because his mechanics did not take short cuts and did things the right way – the Petty way – the first time.

KYLE

I had never seen Richard more excited than when he arrived in Daytona to begin the 1979 season. He had a new role and a new concern. His only worry in previous SpeedWeek visits was getting his car handling well enough and fast enough to win the Daytona 500.

That was still on his agenda.

But this time he was also the father of a young man who was going to begin his racing career at the world's most famous stock-car track, where speeds were in the neighborhood of 200 miles per hour.

"Well, you got to start some place, and I guess this is as good as any," explained 18-year-old Kyle, whose dark curly hair and easy smile reminded everyone of his famous father.

He was entered to drive in the Automobile Racing Club of America race that is run the week before the Daytona 500 every year.

Kyle was only a few months out of Randleman High School, where he played basketball and football. In fact, he was offered college scholarships in both sports but decided he

> **Richard was as nervous as any father would be if his son was going to drive in his first race at Daytona. He was proud, too.**

wanted to race, like his father and grandfather.

It was a natural decision he said. "The family has been in it all my life. Why not? I mean, I could have gone to college and not be having near this much fun."

Richard was as nervous as any father would be if his son was going to drive in his first race at Daytona. He was proud too, and he was the one who had given permission for Kyle to do it.

Kyle's mother, Lynda, was not in favor of having a second driver in the family. "I guess mommas get uptight about things such as this," Kyle explained.

Kyle's car was a Petty-blue Dodge 44. "My grandfather's number was 42. My father's number is 43. It wouldn't add up if I took 45 or something else, would it?" he said.

It figured, too, that Kyle would have more benefits than other youngsters just starting a career. He had a national sponsor, Valvoline, and the best parts, advisors and mechanics, too.

Those were the advantages of being a Petty.

He pointed out that there were drawbacks, too, saying, "If I were Kyle Jones, I could learn for six months and no one would pay any attention to me."

Richard and Kyle had brought the car to Daytona a couple of weeks earlier for a test session, which was the first time that Kyle had ever driven on a high-speed oval.

Kyle did well enough to convince his father that he would not embarrass himself or risk hurting himself seriously in the race.

Still, Richard was totally surprised when Kyle posted the second-fastest qualifying speed to win the outside pole position for the ARCA race.

"I thought if he went 180 miles per hour that he would be doing good," Richard said. "I never would have guessed he would go 189.

Kyle said that he wasn't any more nervous than he was when quarterbacking the Randleman football team. But, like everyone else, he didn't know what to expect from himself in the race.

"I just hope people don't expect me to go out there and win. If I finish last, it would be stupid for anyone to say I couldn't cut it. Even if I win, I shouldn't be judged on my first race."

Dale Inman, who had been with Richard when he started racing, and Kyle's uncle, Maurice, were in his pit on race day.

Richard and other family members watched the race from atop a transporter in the garage area.

Richard's final words to Kyle before the start of the race were those of a father. "Win, lose, or draw – it doesn't matter to me. Just be careful," he said.

Kyle drove a careful race, but it was evident from the start that winning mattered to him. He led eighteen laps until he made his first pit stop.

He was in and out of the lead a couple of times before finding himself second when an accident brought out the caution flag with only seven laps remaining.

Kyle beat Phil Finney back to the line to take the lead for the caution period. When the green flag reappeared with four laps to go, Kyle looked like a veteran as he fought off a last-lap challenge from John Rezak, the pole-sitter, to take the checkered flag.

Richard climbed down from the truck and was on pit road to greet his son following the cool-down lap.

He jumped into the car to congratulate Kyle, and told him, "You did a super, super job. If someone had written a Hollywood script, it wouldn't have ended this good."

Lee Petty summed it best, though, when he said, "Three weeks ago we didn't even know if Kyle could change gears in a race car."

Lee was grinning as if he had just dropped a 50-foot birdie putt, and I couldn't remember ever seeing Richard happier about winning a race himself.

The next day, when I visited the garage area, I found veterans of the sport just as amazed by what Kyle had done as were the fans and reporters.

"It is just unbelievable," said Jake Elder, one of the circuit's top crew chiefs. "Nobody has ever done what he did before, and you probably won't ever see it again, either."

After Kyle's victory, everyone had quickly

asked when he would make his first Winston Cup start. "You can't drive for Richard Petty until you are twenty-one," Kyle replied.

That was what Richard told him before the victory. When asked about it, Richard grinned and said, "I just told him that to get him off my back."

Elder thought Kyle had showed enough in the ARCA race to immediately compete on NASCAR's top circuit.

"I'd say one year from now, he could be winning races on the Winston Cup tour," Elder predicted. "I think the old man (Lee) will talk to Richard and tell him to get the boy started. The boy is going to be a driver, I'm telling you. It is born in him. He is a Petty."

Richard knew it would be hard to keep Kyle out of a race car. "I can't tell him anymore that he doesn't know how to drive. He's done showed he can drive well enough to win."

A.J. Foyt was another who complimented Kyle's driving talent, and he knew there was more there than just being Richard Petty's son.

Foyt explained to me that his son, Tony, was interested in only racing horses, not cars, because he didn't want to see anyone get hurt.

"I am sure Kyle was born with a little ability, and he listened to what his father, grandfather, and uncle told him. He did one helluva job. He had a level head, and when he got in trouble a couple of times he knew how to get out of it," Foyt said.

"Kyle could be one of your next stars on the NASCAR circuit. I know Richard has got to be real proud of him."

Richard gives Kyle some advice during his rookie season.

Elder and a few others suggested that Richard ought to just retire and leave the racing to Kyle. "There is nothing left for Richard to accomplish. He's got himself a driver now, and he could just take it easy," Elder said.

Kyle knew that was not going to happen. "If Daddy didn't still love racing so much, he might think about quitting. But he loves it as much as he always has, and I don't see him quitting in the next several years," Kyle said.

Kyle was right, of course, and Elder was wrong when he said there was nothing left for Richard to accomplish.

Not to be upstaged by his teen-aged son, King Richard won his sixth Daytona 500 the following Sunday, and went from there to win his seventh national championship.

Not only was he still the King. He was still the Number One driver in his family, too.

DIAMONDS AND BLUE FINGERNAILS

Daytona 500 week is always an exciting time for stock car fans.

It is the next best thing to a robin's chirp to signal that winter is almost over, and northern race fans can begin adjusting to warmer temperatures by visiting Daytona International Speedway for SpeedWeeks in February.

More exciting than anything, though, is that Daytona signals the start of a new NASCAR season as engines roar to life and teams roll out their new model race cars.

During the early 1970's, Richard Petty added his own personalized flair to that excitement.

Not only did race fans want to get their first glimpse of the new Petty race car, but they wanted to see, too, what new look King Richard would bring with him to Daytona.

This was before Richard had adopted what now is his trademark appearance of sunglasses, mustache, and wide-brim cowboy hat.

At the start of his third decade in racing, he

Daytona signals the start of a new NASCAR season as engines roar to life and teams roll out their new model race cars, and during the early 1970s, Richard Petty added his own personalized flair to that excitement.

was still looking for that right appearance.

One year he arrived in Daytona with sideburns long enough to shame another king, Elvis. "I grew them when we raced out in California," he told me. "If you don't have long hair out there, you feel naked."

The next year, he arrived with a Fu Manchu mustache, an indication that at thirty-five he was still modish in style.

"Back during the winter all my mechanics and myself started letting our beards grow," Richard said. "We were spending fifteen or more hours a day building the new cars, and we really didn't have time to do anything but work and sleep."

"When it came time to go to Daytona, the others cut their beards and I was the one who didn't."

The Fu Manchu, worn under a black moonshiner's hat, was not accepted warmly by his fans. They thought it made their hero look too much like a villain.

The following year, in 1974, Richard arrived in Daytona looking like Mr. Clean. Gone were the long sideburns and the Fu Manchu. I told him he looked five years younger.

"My wife, Lynda, cleaned me up," Richard responded.

A couple of years later, Richard was back in Daytona with a full beard this time. It must have been another long, hard-working winter.

In the next few years, Richard put on the cowboy hat, sunglasses, and grew a conventional mustache that would become his trademark for the remainder of his driving career.

By that time, son Kyle was the one turning heads in the garage area, and never so much as in the summer of 1983.

Shortly after arriving at the Daytona track for the July race, I needed to talk to Kyle about a story I was writing, and I asked one of his mechanics where he might be.

"Check the powder room," I was told.

The powder room?

It turned out that the macho-image of NASCAR racing was about to take a beating, and Kyle was cracking the whip.

Kyle, the son of the toughest race car driver of them all, had showed up for the Daytona race with a twinkle in his ear instead of his eyes.

The young Petty was the first stock-car driver to have his ear pierced and wear an earring. It was a small diamond. Really kinda cute, too.

"He had a small gold one," explained Richard, who didn't seem the least bit embarrassed by it all. "But his wife didn't like it, and they went to town and bought the diamond."

Kyle, who joined the conversation, said his wife didn't care much for the diamond one either. "But my momma and grandma like it. So does everyone else, too."

Mechanic Mike Beam looked up from under the hood of Kyle's car and shot back, "Not everyone. I just hope he doesn't show up to drive in a fire-proof dress!"

Kyle smiled, without blushing.

"I told him not to worry unless I started driving in culottes," he said.

When Kyle left, I asked Richard what he really thought about the earring.

"I haven't said much about it," he replied. "He's got to do his own thing. He's not following in Richard Petty's footsteps. He tries to be different, and have his own identity. That is good."

The story of Kyle's pierced ear began in Atlanta a couple of months earlier. He and a few friends passed an ear-piercing shop while on the way to a movie. They planned to get their ears pierced after the movie, but by then the shop was closed.

"So, last month when we were racing in Michigan, I was in a mall and a girl was piercing ears for eight dollars. I got my left ear pierced, so it cost me only four bucks," Kyle said.

Men wearing earrings had begun to catch on in the big cities, but back home in Randleman, it was not yet high fashion.

Still Richard thought it might catch on. After all, he said, Kyle had a history of liberalizing the small town's fashion trends.

"When he was in high school and used to go with us when I raced in California, he'd see what all those West Coast cats were doing and bring it back to North Carolina," Richard said.

"Once when he was eleven or twelve he went out there when everyone was starting to wear long hair. He came back, let his hair grow, and pretty soon most of the other boys in his school had long hair, too."

He must have made an impression on the town's racing hero, too, because that would have been the year Richard brought his Fu Manchu to Daytona.

Richard said that when he was growing up he tried to copy his father. "He was my hero, and I tried to do everything he did. Kids growing up today are different. Circumstances are entirely different, and I think parents have to be versatile enough to understand what the trends are," he said.

Richard figured since he was only twenty-three years older than Kyle that he could still understand him. "At least, I try, because I can remember when I wanted to do stuff that my parents wouldn't let me do," he said.

I agreed with Richard that parents should be open-minded. Then I noticed that one of the fingernails on his left hand was painted a light blue, and wondered if he was taking the "understanding" too far.

Richard laughed.

"Oh, that," he said.

"My daughter bought me a blue swim suit for my birthday. She was painting her nails, and it was the same color of the swim suit. So she painted that fingernail."

"But I tell you what. When I was in high school, I used to paint one of my fingernails red. You know, it was something to do. I guess I wore it that way for about a month."

Most everyone figured that Kyle's diamond wouldn't last forever, either. "When I get everyone aggravated enough, I'll take it off and let my ear close up," Kyle said.

But not everyone was giving Kyle a hard time.

When old-time racer Bob Welborn walked up, Richard asked what he thought about a driver wearing an earring.

Welborn only shrugged and said it didn't matter to him what Kyle had in his ear, but how he drove the car.

"If that had been the trend when I was growing up, I probably would have been the first to wear one," Welborn added.

Really, I think Welborn might have been more concerned about Richard's blue fingernail polish than Kyle's diamond.

POPULAR PETTY

Richard Petty never dreamed when he began his racing career that he would become the biggest winner or the most popular driver in the sport's history. If becoming famous had been his goal, he certainly would have selected some other sport or profession, because in the late 1950s no one could predict that stock car racing and its competitors would enjoy such widespread popularity.

Of all the questions asked Richard, probably the most difficult for him to explain is the reason for his immense popularity, which continued to grow even after he stopped winning. He suggests he came into the sport at the right time and grew with it. He was at the front of the pack of a new generation of drivers who took over from pioneer stars such as Buck Baker, Joe Weatherly, Curtis Turner, the Flock Brothers and his own father.

Richard thinks it helped that he was driving a Plymouth during his early years. "There were a lot of Ford fans and a lot of Chevrolet fans, and

If he had been a factory worker, a farmer, or a country mechanic, Richard Petty still would have been popular among those who knew him.

if their favorite driver dropped out of the race, the Chevrolet fan was not going to pull for a Ford driver, and the Ford fan was not going to pull for a Chevrolet driver. But they didn't mind seeing a Plymouth driver win," Richard explained.

Maybe that had something to do with it.

But I believe the overwhelming factor was Richard himself.

If he had been a factory worker, a farmer, or a country mechanic, Richard still would have been popular among those who knew him. He is just downright likable, and he never allowed the success he had to spoil him.

The only other sports superstars who attracted so much popularity and enjoyed the relationship with their fans so much as does Richard were golf's Arnold Palmer and basketball's Julius Erving. But even they eventually outgrew their fans and did not give them same considerations as Richard.

Will Rogers once said he never met a person he did not like. Well, I cannot remember ever meeting anyone who did not like Richard Petty, the person. By that, I mean there were plenty of fans who cheered for other drivers, but they still admired and respected the man that Richard was.

Likewise, I do not recall ever reading a negative story about Richard, and that is not something that can be said about any other celebrity who has been in the public eye for several decades.

I do remember one Atlanta sports writer who seemed determined to be the first to write a critical story about stock car racing's popular King. He had never been to a race, and his reporting experience was in other professional sports. He did not believe a superstar could be all that Richard was made out to be. The writer asked and received permission to write what he said would be the first "totally objective" story about Richard. When the circuit arrived in Atlanta, the writer went to the speedway and interviewed Richard, as well as other drivers and race officials.

Then he returned to his office to write his "totally objective" story. It turned out to be one of the most complimentary stories anyone ever wrote about Richard.

The writer learned, as had I and others who covered the sport, that Richard was as genuine as his smile, a man who did not shed one personality and put on another when the cameras or note pads were put away.

Mike Harris likes telling about the first time he was sent to cover a Winston Cup race after being named the motorsports writer for the Associated Press.

"I didn't know anyone on the NASCAR cir-cuit, because most of my experience had been with Indianapolis drivers," Harris says. "I decided the best thing to do was to start at the top."

That, of course, meant visiting King Richard.

"I had heard that in addition to being the most famous driver on the circuit, Richard was the easiest to approach," Harris continues. "But I could not believe how nice he was. After five minutes it was like we had known each other most of our lives. After an hour we were talking about members of our families."

Many others have left that initial visit with Richard with the same memory. It didn't matter, either, if the writer was from the Associated Press or a small town publication. Richard was the same with everyone.

Deb Williams, an editor for Winston Cup Scene and a writer for other national publications, feels she has known Richard all of her life. She grew up a race fan near Asheville, N.C., and Richard was her first hero. Her father had pulled for Lee Petty, and she felt it was only natural for her to cheer for Richard.

One of the downsides to being a sports writer is that when you get a chance to meet and get to know one of your childhood heroes, you often are disappointed to discover a different person than you had thought him to be.

That did not happen when Williams got to know Richard, first professionally and then as friends with him and his wife, Lynda.
Richard says no athlete ever had a better relationship with the media, and I agree with him.

"I have been in some controversial incidents, but I think the press did a fair job of reporting them," he says. "It wasn't that the press took my side all the time, but the writers told what I had to say and left it at that. I am not saying that I agreed with everything that was written about me, but I think overall the press tried to be fair."

Richard enjoyed the same type of relationship with his fans. No one remembers him ever being rude, and he seemed always to have time for autograph requests unless he was rushing to keep an appointment.

I have seen some drivers at autograph sessions sign their names for fans who waited in line for hours to meet them and never looked up or said hello. Not Richard, who had a smile and a greeting for everyone. More times than not he would thank the fan for wanting his autograph.

Unlike many other superstars, Richard never attended a session where fans would be charged to get his autograph. He once was scheduled for an appearance in Portsmouth, Va., but quickly canceled out when he learned that fans would have to pay to get his autograph. Another driver was brought in to take his place.

At times when I complimented Richard on his patience and dedication to his fans, he frequently reminded me that he also benefited from being so cooperative with the media and the public.

"Sometimes it is a necessary evil," he said. "I don't mind it at all if the car is running good and there are no problems. But if there is a problem with the car, that is on my mind. I want the media and the fans to give me my time to solve those problems, and then I will give them their time for what they want."

Richard believed he was working for the fans, too. They were the ones who bought the tickets to watch him race. They were the ones who purchased his sponsors' products, so he could have the money to race. "Anything you want to do, somewhere along the way you have to pay for it," Richard said.

"When I take the time to do an interview or sign an autograph, I feel as if I am paying part of the bill for being able to race. Eventually, it will come home."

I admit I have seen Richard become irritated on race mornings when fans found their way into the garage area and inconsiderately interrupted him to ask for an autograph or to pose with them for a snapshot while he was in the process of getting ready for a race. But the only signs of irritation were expressed after he signed the autograph or smiled for the snapshot and the happy fan had left.

I have seen some fans feel slighted when they called to Richard from a few feet away when he failed to turn and acknowledge them. But it was doubtful if Richard ever heard them, since his hearing has been severely weakened by engine noise through the years.

For the most part, I think Richard enjoys signing autographs because of the happiness it brings to his fans.

Charlotte Motor Speedway president H.A. Wheeler recalls once before a race he was stopped by a man who said he had driven from Roanoke, Va., to Rockingham, N.C., to get Richard's autograph for his nine-year-old son who was dying with cancer. The boy's last wish was to get Richard's autograph.

Wheeler did not know if the man was serious, or just wanted to get Richard's autograph.

But he went to the garage and asked Richard to sign the card the man had given him. Richard signed it and also an STP cap.

"I took the card and the cap back to the grandstand, where the man was waiting," Wheeler says. "The man started crying and thanked me profusely. He turned around and left, and my eyes followed him to the parking lot where he got in his car and headed north."

I remember being stopped one race morning at Atlanta by a small boy in a wheelchair, who asked if I could get Richard's autograph for him. I told Richard about the request, and he nodded, but did not sign the piece of paper so I could return it to the youngster. He was in a meeting, which lasted a few more minutes, and then he took the paper himself to where the young fan was waiting. He gave him an autograph and, more importantly, several minutes of his time.

Despite all the autographs he had signed during his lengthy career, Richard seemed still to be amazed by the long lines that formed during his many personal appearances on his Fan Appreciation Tour. "People will stand in line for hours to get my autograph, and then thank me. All I do is sit there and sign. I should be the one thanking them," he said.

ALL THE KING'S CHARIOTS

The most exotic-looking race car ever to race on the Winston Cup circuit was the 1970 Plymouth Superbird. It looked like it was going 200 miles per hour standing still. The car was long and lean with a smooth, blade-like nose and a wing above the trunk. Of all the cars that Richard drove during his career, he says the '70 Superbird was the best. Surrounded by many of Richard's trophies, the car occupies center stage at the Petty museum.

The 1970 Plymouth Superbird was a car fit for a king. And most of us believed it was built especially for the King of stock car racing.

It was a car fit for a king. And most of us believed it was built especially for the King of stock car racing.

Ford Motor Company and Chrysler Corporation were at war on the nation's race tracks in those days. "The car that wins on Sunday sells on Monday" became a popular saying, and there were impressive statistics, especially in the southern market, to support such a contention.

In the first decade of his career, Richard was not only Plymouth's best salesman, he was the number one Ford beater on the NASCAR circuit.

He did not begin his career in a Plymouth. He drove an Oldsmobile in nineteen races before driving a Plymouth for the first time to finish 26th in the 1959 Firecracker 250 at Daytona. He went back to the Oldsmobile for another three races before returning to a Plymouth to establish his reputation as King Richard.

Richard collected his first 92 victories in Plymouths. Like the Petty-blue color and the Number 43, Plymouth was something of a Petty tradition. None of us ever thought we would see Richard driving anything else.

But in 1968, Richard became disenchanted with the Chrysler racing bosses. He knew the future of Petty Enterprises did not rest on him driving Plymouths, but on winning races, and he did not think Chrysler was giving him the support he needed to race the strong Fords in 1969.

"Take it or leave it," Chrysler big-wigs told the Pettys.

For Richard, it was like going downtown to buy a new car. You listened to what this salesman had to say, and if you didn't like it, you went across the street and tried to get a better deal.

He went down the street to the Ford factory, where he was presented a winning deal. "The whole Petty family knew we had to change to a Ford to be competitive in 1969," Richard explained. "It was strictly business."

Some of Richard's Plymouth fans were sorely disappointed, and he even heard a few boos the first time his brought his 1969 Ford Torino to a southern race track. But most of the just plain ol' Petty fans understood and reserved their anger for the Chrysler people who had let Richard get away.

Richard debuted the Ford at Riverside, Calif., in the Motor Trend 500. He started fourth and finished first. He won eight other races during the 1969 season while the few teams that remained with Chrysler products struggled with outclassed equipment.

Chrysler executives did not enjoy getting beat so thoroughly on the speedways, and the defection of Richard, which affected car sales in the South, was another sore spot. Building a car that would get the King back became a major goal.

The Superbird was just such a chariot, and Petty fans everywhere were smiling to see him back in a Plymouth for the 1970 season. "Welcome home, Richard," read one banner in the grandstands during Daytona 500 week.

"I am not an emotional person, but I feel more at home in a Plymouth," Richard said. "How to explain it, I really don't know."

Richard never regretted the switch to Ford for the 1969 season. The move back to the Chrysler camp was the right one at the right time, too, as Ford decided during the 1970 season to reduce drastically its stock car racing program.

Richard again was lucky enough to do the right thing at the right time. And it was luck because he had no indication when he jumped back to Chrysler that Ford was preparing to trim its role in racing.

Chrysler replied to Ford's cutbacks in 1971, when it fielded only two factory teams, both out of the Petty stable. Richard drove the Superbird and Buddy Baker drove a winged-Dodge. The next year, Richard jumped back and forth between a Plymouth and a Dodge before driving his final victory in a Plymouth at North Wilkesboro Speedway on October 1, 1972.

"The Superbird was the best race car I ever drove, but the car I liked best was the '72 Dodge because we used it for five or six years," Richard says.

He was forced by the rules finally to give up the '72-style Dodge in 1978, the season in which he made the most publicized car switch in NASCAR history. Sure, the move from a Plymouth to a Ford in 1969 was a shocker, but it came between seasons.

The Petty team's switch from a Dodge to a Chevrolet Monte Carlo in the middle of the 1978 season ranks as one of the greatest accomplishments in the sport.

Richard's mechanics had to continue preparing the Dodge for a busy schedule while at the same time building a new line of cars with which they were totally unfamiliar. When Richard made the move to Ford, that factory supplied him with the best equipment and technology. This time, the Petty camp went it alone. "We've got to do in four weeks what the other Chevy teams have had four years to do," Richard explained at the time.

The switch to a Chevrolet was not only back-breaking, it was dollar-busting, too.

The Pettys had invested hundreds of thousands of dollars into trying to get the new-model Dodge Magnum competitive, and that was money down a hole.

Still, when the middle of the season appeared just over the fourth turn wall, Richard made the only decision he could.

"My sponsor, STP, expects us to win races, and they don't care if it is in a Dodge or a Volkswagen," Richard had told me at North Wilkesboro in April. "If we don't start winning, they might not be around next year."

Richard felt that NASCAR was not interested in keeping a Dodge racing on its circuit. He had told sanctioning body officials what adjustments to the rules needed to be made so the Dodge would be competitive with the General Motors cars that were dominating the season. There were precedents, he said. NASCAR once had taken the hemi engines away from the Chrysler teams, and it had declared the SuperBird illegal for competition.

While it did not seem important to NASCAR for Richard to win another race in a Dodge, it was important to him to win another race—period. The decision to change to a Chevrolet was finalized in a family meeting at Daytona in July and had the strong endorsement of Lee Petty.

"Daddy wants to win," Richard told me. "He doesn't believe in anything else."

Again, Petty fans for the most part understood the decision. Richard figured that 40 per cent of the fans understood, and another 50 percent didn't care what he was driving. For the other 10 percent, Richard tried to explain, even writing personal letters to some.

"I just told them that I had to make a living out of this stuff, and had tried the best I could to make the Dodge competitive before making the switch," he said.

He drove the Dodge for the final time in the Talladega 500 on August 6, 1978, to a seventh-place finish.

Richard debuted the Chevrolet in the Champion 400 at Michigan International Speedway on August 20, 1978. "What you are looking at is a three-week miracle," Richard told us as we inspected the Number 43 Chevy in its garage stall.

Everyone was surprised that the car performed as well as it did. Richard was running near the front when a cut tire caused him to crash into the wall on the backstretch.

Richard drove mostly Chevrolets for the next two seasons. He drove an Oldsmobile at some of the superfast tracks, including Daytona, where in 1979 he became the first driver to win the 500 in an Oldsmobile since Lee Petty in 1959.

Richard, who became the first driver to win the Daytona 500 in a Buick in 1981, made his final switch to a Pontiac in 1982. The Pontiac in which he collected his 200th career victory in 1984 is on permanent display in the Smithsonian Institute in Washington.

Cars and Crews

1971

1972

1973

Cars and Crews

1992

Cars and Crews

Pit row, where races are sometimes won or lost, requires total communication between driver and crew. In top photo, Richard waits for signal from crew chief Dale Inman. "I don't care whether they beat on the car, yell or what; until I get the sign from Dale, the car doesn't move," Richard says.

Cars and Crews

Richard's pit crew goes to work.

Cars and Crews

In 1979, Richard won his seventh championship. His pit crew, led by Maurice (third from left, won the National Pit Crew championship. Kyle (second from left) also was a member of the crew.

Cars and Crews

Crewmen inspect the damage during a pit stop in the 1992 Daytona 500.

POLITICS

He is a tall, thin man who was born in poverty, grew up a hero of the common man and felt perfectly comfortable in the White House.

Abraham Lincoln?

Nope. Richard Petty.

Richard was born in his grandparents' house on July, 2, 1937. It was a house without running water or electricity. "It was poverty," Lee Petty says.

And although Richard didn't grow up to be president, he did become a "king," and frequently during his career he was the guest at state dinners in the White House.

In 1978, when Jimmy Carter, a longtime race fan, was president, he invited the whole Winston Cup circuit for a picnic on the South Lawn of the White House. Richard was the one that we went to with our questions about what to expect.

We knew that Richard, a staunch Republican, had been there a couple of times previously as a guest of President Richard Nixon.

For one thing, Richard said, it was all right to wear boots with your suit or tux if you wanted.

In 1978, when President Jimmy Carter invited the whole Winston Cup circuit for a picnic at the White House, Richard was the one we went to with our questions about what to expect.

That was the beginning to a humorous story that Richard tells on himself about the first time he and Lynda were invited to the White House.

"Lynda was all excited, and she had made sure to get all the proper stuff for us to wear," Richard said. "Well, I got my tuxedo on, and I started putting my boots on. Lynda about had a fit. She told me that I couldn't go the White House wearing my boots. I told her that I went to church with my boots on. I went racing with my boots on. And I was going to dinner at the White House with my boots on, too."

Richard figured just because he was going to be the dinner guest of the president of the United States that he should not try to be something he wasn't. "The president is just like me," Richard said. "The only difference is our jobs."

President Carter missed his own party because of summit talks he was conducting at Camp David between Egyptian President Sadat and Israeli Prime Minister Begin. The president's wife, Rosalynn, told us that it would take something of the "utmost importance" to keep her husband away from the party.

Having talked racing with Mr. Carter before he was elected president, I am sure this was true, too. He had waved the green flag for a race at Atlanta while only a candidate, and he promised if elected he would be the first president to invite the stock car crowd to dinner.

The cars of Bobby Allison, Benny Parsons, David Pearson and Cale Yarborough were parked on the far corner of the White House lawn. Richard was unable to bring his car because it was still being prepared for the following Sunday's race at Dover, Del.

The Pettys were well-represented, though. Richard brought Lynda and his daddy. Maurice and Dale Inman brought their wives. Most of the drivers were given abbreviated tours of the White House, and Richard was escorted into the Oval Office.

"I have been here before, but this is the first time I have really felt comfortable," he said.

Richard himself had gotten into local politics back home in Randolph County during the spring of 1978 when he was elected to run on the Republican ticket for a seat on the county commission. When I talked to him about it, he described the primary as a "heat race."

I reminded him that politics, on any level, could get down and dirty. Did he have any skeletons in his closet, I kiddingly asked.

"You couldn't put all the skeletons I got into a closet unless it was an awfully big one," he replied. "But I probably still don't have as many as the others."

Richard was as serious about the political race as he could be, and it was his nature to want to do it the right way. I remember he was puzzled about how much money he should use for his campaign. He didn't want people to say he had spent so much that he bought the election. On the other hand, he didn't want to spend too little and have people thinking he didn't have to campaign or advertise because he was Richard Petty.

Petty won the election in the fall, and he admitted he did not know if people had voted for him because he was a famous race driver or not. "I just asked them to vote for me, and I didn't ask them why if they did," he explained.

Ask Richard when he first became interested in politics, and he is likely to reply when he became a race driver. Indeed, there is a lot of politicking involved in being a winning driver on the Winston Cup circuit, and Richard seemed always in the middle of it.

In addition to campaigning for favorable rules, Richard was president of the short-lived Professional Drivers Association, which was formed in 1969 and was the only legitimate driver's organization on the Winston Cup circuit.

Richard was at the front of the line, too, when the PDA elected to not compete in the inaugural race at Alabama International Motor Speedway, which NASCAR founder Bill France, Sr., built. An angry France threatened to ban Richard from the NASCAR circuit, as he had done with Curtis Turner years earlier for trying to form a union.

But France was wise enough not to begin a legal war with the biggest draw that his circuit had, and the PDA eventually expired of natural causes.

I think that Richard's running for local office

the first time had a lot to do with someone putting up a "Welcome Race Fans" banner, with an STP emblem, across the front of a so-called massage parlor just inside Randolph County.

The folks in neighboring Guilford County had passed ordinances that drove such questionable business across the line, which was not far away from Level Cross. The Pettys took care of getting that STP "welcome" banner removed, but Richard believed the county needed leaders who would provide for "more orderly growth."

During the 1980 Republican presidential primary, both Ronald Reagan and John Connally courted Richard and met with him and Lynda to outline their views. Richard stayed mostly on the white line in that contest, pointing out that he mainly wanted to help the party beat the Democrats.

When President Reagan ran for reelection in 1984, he again sought Richard's support. But he learned there was more to getting an endorsement from Richard Petty than from most of the other celebrities lining up behind him.

Richard wasn't just going to give a blanket endorsement. He and Lynda met alone with the president for more than an hour. They talked about education, foreign policy, defense and other topics. When the meeting broke up, I am not sure who was the most impressed by whom.

Richard once described his political leanings to me as being "a little to the right of Jesse Helms," the North Carolina Republican who is one of the most conservative members of the U.S. Senate. Richard doesn't believe in government giveaways, but he supports a strong defense and solid education programs.

Such a platform seemingly would make him a strong candidate for any office he desired in North Carolina, and most of us who had known Richard for a long time always agreed that when he ended his driving career he should run for the U.S. Senate or the governor's office.

Racing was always first with Richard, but politics seemed a distant second, and a long way from whatever was third. During down periods on race weeks, he could sit in the back of his truck for hours and discuss issues ranging from those in his own county to international matters.

If Petty Enterprises had been in better competitive shape when Richard decided to end his driving career, maybe he would have launched an immediate political career. But there was too much unfinished work that Richard had to do with directing the rebuilding of the Petty team for him to do that at the end of the 1992 season.

Still, I would be very surprised if we do not see Richard running for a state office in the next few years, and as in racing, I don't think he would settle for anything but a top position.

In the late '80s, the North Carolina Republicans attempted to get Richard to run for lieutenant governor, and I think they got the message then that he is not a guy who is willing to settle for being Number 2.

Richard told them he figured he could get elected governor as easily as he could lieutenant governor.

And what about his lack of experience in state politics?

"I might not know what is going on, but them other cats don't seem to, either," Richard said.

THE WAY IT WAS IN '78

Richard Petty was getting ready to leave his house to go a race at Martinsville, Va., in 1971 when he said goodbye to his six-year-old daughter Sharon and got the strangest reply.

"I hope you don't win, Daddy," Sharon said.

Suspecting mutiny in his household, Richard did a quick about-face and demanded an explanation.

"The house is going fall in if you keep winning those races," his wide-eyed daughter said.

Richard laughed about her remark later that day, after winning one more time at the half-mile Martinsville track, just across the North Carolina line and only about a 90-minute drive from the Petty shop.

"I keep all my trophies in the attic, and there is a crack along the ceiling under the attic," he said. "Sharon told me she was afraid if I won any more trophies the ceiling was going to collapse."

Winning was a way of life for the Petty family during those good ol' days. "When I was a lit-

As low as Richard felt during the 1973 season, when he finished with six victories, it was nothing compared to the 1978 season, when for the first time in 19 years, he failed to win a race.

tle boy, we always thought Daddy was going to win every race there was," says Kyle.

But only a couple of years after Sharon's fears that all of Richard's trophies were going to bring down the house, Richard seemed to get a feeling that he could not dominate the stock car road forever.

He came into the 1973 Southern 500 with only four victories and $150,945 in prize money. Most drivers would have been delighted with those figures. But they were not satisfactory for King Richard, who had his own standards.

He definitely was not pleased with his season when I talked to him a day before the Darlington race.

"I could win the rest of the races on the schedule and it still would not be a good year for me," he said. "I have to judge myself on my best marks, and I am way short of them."

Richard's career highs for a season were $300,000 in prize money and 27 victories. I reminded him that when he won 27 races in 1967 there were more than 50 races on the schedule. Now there were only 32.

"Don't make any difference," Richard said. "You still have to judge yourself on what you did before and try to improve on that."

Richard's problem during 1973 was mostly mechanical. He figured he didn't finish about half of the races and he blamed most of that on NASCAR playing politics with the rulebook.

"I can't ever remember getting outrun as bad as I have this year," he said. "The more I get outrun, the more we try to experiment to come up with something that will help out. You wind up stretching the limitations of the engine and the equipment, and the strain hurts."

While Richard was expressing his frustrations, someone walked up and accidentally addressed him as "Pearson."

It was a bad mistake at a bad time.

Richard smiled weakly and pointed to the pink thread that scrawled his name on his driving uniform.

"I used to wear an uniform that didn't have a name on it," he said. "That was back when I was winning and everyone knew who I was. Now, I have to wear this uniform with my name on it."

Bobby Allison, listening in on the conversation, grinned and said, "It is getting a little faded, isn't it?"

Richard faked a hard look at Allison and said, "You mean the uniform or the reputation?"

As low as Richard felt in the 1973 season, which he finished with six victories, it was nothing compared to the 1978 season, when for the first time 19 years, he failed to win a race.

The biggest problem that season was not that Richard was losing anything as a driver. He simply had stayed too long with Chrysler, which did not have a competitive body style for the NASCAR circuit. It was a situation that chief rival David Pearson and other insiders understood, even if they delighted in needling Richard.

Pearson was in a slump, too, and we talked at Talladega about the problems he and Richard were having.

"I have had some bad luck, and my car isn't as good as it used to be," David said with a straight face. "But Richard...well, to tell you the truth, Richard is just over the hill."

Suddenly, Pearson broke into laughter.

"No," he said, "I can understand Richard's problem. I have not run good since we had to change body styles with the Mercury two years ago. Now Richard is going through the same thing with the new Dodge. He is fighting the same thing I've fought the last two years."

I asked if he missed the excitement of racing Richard for victories.

"Well, I am still racing Richard. We're just farther back in the field. But, yeah, it is frustrating when someone thunders around you and you know they aren't that good."

Richard proved to his satisfaction that the difference between his Dodge and the General Motors cars that were winning the races was the problem when he relieved for Chevrolet driver Lennie Pond during the Bristol race.

"I showed that if I had something to go that I could go with it," Richard said. "I might not be as good as I once was, but in two years I ain't gone from being as good as there ever was to as bad as I am now."

Some of the younger drivers were suggesting that Richard and Pearson both had stronger competition than in the days when they dominated. Such talk infuriated Buddy Baker, who was having his own problems. "When anyone asks me if Richard is over the hill, I tell them that a lot of people would just like to get on that hill to see where Richard Petty has been," Baker said.

"What some people fail to realize is that a driver can't control body styles."

But a driver could change body styles, and that is what Richard did when he traded the Dodge for a Chevrolet in August. The Chevy was much more competitive than the Dodge, but there were other complications to Richard avoiding his first shutout season since 1960.

In the first race with the Chevy at Michigan, he cut a tire late in the race and crashed hard into the wall, cracking several ribs that bothered him during the remainder of the season.

Richard lost an opportunity for a potential victory in late September at Martinsville, where he was a 14-race winner. He put the new Chevy on the outside pole position in qualifying, but halfway through the race he began suffering painful leg cramps and could barely work the brake pedal. Amazingly, he still finished sixth.

Richard had other health problems, too, and following the season, he underwent surgery to have a large portion of his stomach removed.

Considering all the problems of the 1978 season, it was no wonder that even Richard Petty couldn't snare a victory.

But that is not to say he didn't see a checkered flag waving for him. He did, in the next-to-last race of the season in Atlanta.

As Richard's Chevrolet streaked across the finish line, he saw the checkered flag and shouted over the two-way radio to his crewmen, "We did it! We finally won one."

In the stands, thousands of Petty fans danced and clapped their hands.

But as Richard was on his cool-down lap, he heard crew chief Dale Inman saying on the radio, "You didn't win...they are saying Donnie Allison did."

Confused, Richard clicked off the radio and drove his car back to the garage instead of to victory lane. "There is no question about it," he said after exiting his car. "I won the race."

Two hours later, NASCAR agreed with him, and Richard went to the press box. "It has taken me one and a half years and four hours, but I finally won another one," he told us.

Richard answered questions for about 30 minutes. Then he was called to the telephone to get more bad news.

"What?" I heard him say, then repeat it.

He hung up the telephone, turned and shrugged, "Now they are saying I didn't win it."

The fans were angry when the reversal was announced. "Crooks...Crooks...Crooks," they began chanting.

Atlanta Raceway officials seemed just as upset, as were reporters who were having to rewrite their stories for the third time. "This is the biggest bunch of bull that I've ever seen," speedway vice-president Bobby Batson said.

NASCAR president Bill France Jr. said pretty much the same. "It's the biggest foul-up in NASCAR history," France said. "But we are finally as positive as we can be that Donnie

Allison was the winner, and Richard Petty finished second."

For Allison to have won, he had to make up two laps in the final stages of the race. Richard thought Donnie had made up the two laps at one point, but then lost one back during a pit stop. NASCAR officials told him that Donnie was one lap down late in the race.

But the scoring cards showed Allison won the race, and there was nothing Richard could do but accept the decision. He had won and lost a lot of races, but never had he experienced a day like this. In one afternoon he won, lost, won, and finally lost.

"It's kind of frustrating to run all day and then not know where you really finished," he said. "I will always believe that I won."

But in the record book, he was officially listed as 0-for-30 for the 1978 season.

There isn't even an asterisk.

THE HURTIN' PART

If archeologists should come across Richard Petty's remains a thousand years from now, they might believe that this was a man who had been brutally tortured during his life.

How would they know that he had received so much bodily damage doing what he dearly loved, racing?

During his career, Richard has broken his neck twice, broken both shoulders a couple of times, cracked his ribs fifteen times or more, shattered both knees and both feet. He has dislocated his back, banged up his hip, and suffered several concussions.

While most people are amazed that Richard won 200 races, I can't help but wonder how many races and championship he might have won if he hadn't been hurt so much.

Not that he missed entire seasons, or many races at all, because of the injuries and other health problems. Consider the ulcer that prompted major stomach surgery before the 1979 season. Doctors advised Richard to miss the opening race in January at Riverside, Calif., and

During his career, Richard has broken his neck twice, broken both shoulders a couple of times, cracked his ribs 15 times or more, shattered both knees and both feet.

NASCAR officials were worried that he was trying to come back too soon. As usual, he raced anyhow. After the engine blew in his car during the race, Richard climbed out and said, "The engine broke, I didn't." He won the Daytona 500 a few weeks later.

I saw him get in a car at Talladega Superspeedway to start a race with a broken neck in 1980. I have heard Lynda Petty say that even if her husband were dying, if there was a race to be run, he would be there.

The most spectacular and publicized crash of Richard's career was in the 1988 Daytona 500, which was being televised nationally by CBS. Richard's Pontiac was tapped from behind. It flew out of control and virtually disintegrated as it flipped, rolling five times, snagging part of the front grandstand fence, and crashing back onto the track after being hit twice by other cars.

Crew chief Dale Inman ran from pit road and found Richard still conscious. "I'll talk to you when I catch my breath," Richard said. He was taken to a nearby hospital, where he was examined, treated for an ankle injury and released. He was back in his car for the Richmond race the next weekend.

Richard's wreck in the Rebel 400 at Darlington Raceway in 1970 was the scariest I ever saw him have.

I and a lot of others thought he was dead in that one.

Richard's Plymouth smacked the outside fourth turn wall, sped across the track into a thunderous collision with the inside guard rail and began a series of mid-air flips and spins.

Richard's head and left arm could be seen hanging outside the window during the wild ride.

"I thought I saw the car come down on Richard's head, and I thought he was dead," said Ralph Moody, David Pearson's car owner.

As the car settled on its top, Francis Allen, a member of Junior Johnson's crew, dived through a window opening to help Richard.

Allen said Richard was unconscious and hanging in his safety straps. While Allen was working to get him out of the car, Richard came to and said, "Oh, I've hurt my danged shoulder."

He was taken to the infield hospital and the first real sign that he was not critically injured came when Lee Petty emerged from the hospital with a smile on his face.

A short time later, Richard was brought from the building on a stretcher and placed in the ambulance. As fans, some of them weeping, applauded, Richard managed a short wave.

Richard suffered a dislocated shoulder and a few cuts and bruises. A few days later, he came to the race at Hampton, Va., although he was not able to drive. He just wanted to get out and show people he was all right, he told me.

He had been unconscious through most of the wreck and didn't realize how bad it was until he saw pictures of it. "When I was in the hospital, someone asked how many times the car flipped and I thought there had been another wreck. I didn't even realize the car had turned over so many times."

Richard had another brutal crash in 1980 at Pocono, Pa., when a wheel broke while he was leading the race. "I was trying to slam on brakes and turn the steering wheel, but nothing was happening. I saw the white wall that I was about to hit at 150 miles per hour and I told myself, 'Man, this is going to hurt.' "

But Richard, who broke his neck in that one, was not left with any memory of actually feeling pain when he hit the wall. There was a blank spot of four or five seconds in his memory.

"I guess the good Lord doesn't let some of that stuff register," he said. "If we did remember it, we might wake up in the middle of the night screaming."

Most of Richard's crashes were during races, and he had a few days to recover before getting back behind the wheel. But he proved to me just how tough he was after crashing in a Friday practice at Charlotte, spending the night in the hospital, and showing up the next day.

It was on Saturday morning before the 1986 World 600 when the lanky man with the sunglasses, western hat, and cowboy boots came strolling slowly through the garage area gate.

"What's happening?" he asked the security guard.

After a crash at Darlington in 1970, Richard gets checked out by Bill Champion (left) and Dr. Don Tarr.

He was smiling the same broad, pearly smile that was so familiar to us.

We smiled back. It was good to see King Richard back on his feet.

In the previous day's crash, Richard had been knocked unconscious when his car slammed into the third-turn wall. The car caught fire and drove itself back around to the front stretch, with Richard slumped over the steering wheel.

He regained consciousness in the arms of his son, Kyle, who helped to free him from the wrecked car. He was strapped to a stretcher, loaded on a medical helicopter and flown to a Charlotte hospital.

"Tell 'em, to get me a car to drive," he said. "I will be at the track first thing in the morning."

Here he was. Business as usual.

"I am sore," he said. "My dang head hurts."

But he was smiling.

"The doctors said everything was fine, but it was up to me to know if I can drive a race car or not. I am plenty sore and I don't know how much of the race I will be able to drive. But I have been hurt a lot worse than this before and started races."

Richard looked around the garage area for the Petty team truck, but there was only a vacant space where it was once stationed. The truck had carried the remains of his car back to Level Cross.

"Where is my truck?" asked Petty, never breaking his smile. "If I ain't got no truck, I ain't got no place to hang out."

Finally, Richard broke stride, turned and began walking to the corner of the open-air garage, where he found his crewmen busily preparing D.K. Ulrich's Chevrolet for him to drive.

"Let me see my boys," Richard said.

As soon as it had been learned that his car was wrecked beyond repair, Ulrich had offered his Chevrolet for Richard to drive.

"Don't reckon I have ever had a better man driving one of my cars," said D.K. "And when the Petty team gets their engine in the car and makes a few other changes, it will be as good as any car out here."

As Richard approached the car, a middle-aged man stuck out a race cap and asked for an autograph. People can be so inconsiderate at times.

Richard never gave it a second thought. He took the cap, paused and scrawled the most famous signature in racing, then made it official by adding "43" at the end.

After a brief conference with Dale Inman, Richard gently crawled through the window of D.K.'s green and white race car. He gripped the steering wheel with his right hand, then with his left hand.

He reminded me of a kid climbing behind the steering wheel of the new family car for the first time.

Richard held the wheel firmly, shook it back and forth, and said, "Unnnnnnnn... unnn.... unnnn."

A taller man than Ulrich, Richard's knees buckled under the steering wheel. "Got to move the seat back," he told Inman. "It might be a good seat for watching television but not for racin.' "

For the 434th consecutive Winston Cup race,

Richard was going to go racin' when the green flag dropped the next day.

The Pettys are that way because racin' is in their blood.

Only a few minutes after helping his daddy out of the race car on Friday, Kyle was back in his own race car, speeding down the backstretch and right by the third-turn wall that bore the black marks where his daddy had hit.

He was a racer, like his daddy, and he had to get back to preparing himself and the car for Sunday's race. "When I am here at the track, my job is to drive that car," Kyle said. "Daddy understands that. You can't let your emotions override what you are here for. You don't just abandon the ship if something goes wrong. You salvage what you can."

Maurice Petty, Richard's brother and long-time engine builder, understood, too. Before Richard arrived at the track, Maurice shook his head when I asked if the crash might be enough to put retirement thoughts into Richard's head.

"Richard can still drive a race car," Maurice said. "And, he's got a hard head."

THAT LAST CHAMPIONSHIP SEASON

A revolution of sorts was brewing in Richard's kingdom in 1979, the likes of which had not been seen since the early 1960s when youngsters such as Richard, David Pearson, Cale Yarborough and Buddy Baker began infiltrating the ranks of the old-guard heroes.

Newcomers on the circuit included Bill Elliott, a red-haired, Huck Finn look-a-like from the north Georgia mountains; Dale Earnhardt, a hard-driving North Carolinian; and Darrell Waltrip, a brash, smooth-talking Tennessean who some people were saying was the most apparent heir to Richard's throne.

It seemed strange to me that Waltrip was being compared to Richard, because their personalities were so different. But even Richard pointed out some similarities about their careers.

"Darrell benefits from coming into the sport at the right time, when there is a changing of the guard. I did the same thing in the 1960s, moving up when people like Daddy, Buck Baker, Fireball Roberts, and Junior Johnson were fading out of the picture."

> **Even during his richest seasons, Richard never saw himself as being on a different level from everyone else in the garage area.**

Richard, though, blended into the circuit and never declared his intentions of busting records or becoming king of the road. Even during his richest seasons, he never saw himself as being on a different level from everyone else in the garage area. He was appreciative of the records and contributions drivers before him had made to the sport.

Darrell Waltrip, brimming with talent, ego, and ambition, was another kind of cat, as Richard often noted.

He was the first young driver that I had seen to come on the circuit with the announced intentions of taking over from the King. He belittled Richard's records, saying for the most part that they were set on cow-pasture tracks against questionable competition.

The first time I recall Richard becoming seriously irritated with Waltrip was at Charlotte Motor Speedway in the summer of 1978, when the Pettys were battling the frustrations of trying to make the Dodge Magnum competitive.

Richard, Dale and Maurice had worked long

and hard on a few new tricks in preparing the Dodge for the Charlotte race, but their efforts became fruitless when NASCAR refused to approve the car during inspection. Neither NASCAR nor Richard cared to specify exactly what was not right with the car, but the Petty crew loaded up and took it back to Level Cross to correct the problem.

Needless to say, Richard was not in the proper mood to have someone making fun of the situation when the team returned with the car the next day. But Waltrip, who already had a reputation for having a sharp wit, couldn't resist.

Waltrip thought the rear trunk of the Dodge was too long, and it didn't seem to him that the Pettys had made any big changes after taking it back to Level Cross.

"If they fixed it, they only halfway fixed it," Waltrip said. "I heard the car was about four inches too long. I can still look at the car and tell it is not right.

"That trunk looks so big, I bet he could get a lot of luggage in it. You reckon he's trying to get a sponsorship from Samsonite? It looks to me like he would have lengthened the front of the car. That's the part that crosses the finish line first."

As I expected, Richard did not find Waltrip's observations the least bit humorous. The needle stung. He didn't like it, and I am sure he didn't forget it for a long time. "I don't mind debating an issue with someone who can compete, but I am not going to argue with people such as him," Richard told me.

A season later, in 1979, Waltrip, the young lion, and Petty, the aging king, locked up in a duel for the Winston Cup championship that became the tightest points battle in stock car racing history.

Early in the year, it seemed the title bout would be between Waltrip and Bobby Allison, another veteran who did not appreciate the youngster's brashness. Then it seemed there wouldn't be much of a title race at all.

Waltrip won at Talladega on August 5 to build a 229-point lead over Richard, who was second in the standings. No one had ever squandered such a big lead with only ten races left.

But Petty, the old pro, got stronger as the season rolled on, and Waltrip, in his first title run, showed his inexperience.

Scoring victories at Michigan, Dover, and Rockingham during a sizzling run, Richard took an eight-point lead over Waltrip with only the Atlanta and Ontario, Calif., races remaining.

Waltrip resented Richard saying that he was feeling the pressure of the championship run, and he even accused NASCAR of favoring his opponent. "Everyone is telling me I lost the big lead because I couldn't handle it," he said. "It is kinda like one of those Hollywood movies where everyone goes around telling a guy he is crazy. Pretty soon he thinks he is crazy."

Waltrip also was clearly envious of all the media attention that Petty was stirring in his bid to win his seventh national championship. He quickly ended one interview with me and a couple of other writers when he saw Richard approaching.

"Well, here comes the King," he said. "Let this poor, second-class sonofagun get out of here."

Richard, meanwhile, was a picture of cool behind his dark sunglasses and long, thin cigar. When someone asked if he felt any pressure, he smiled. "How do you spell that word?" he asked.

It didn't seem to ruffle him either that Waltrip finished fifth, one position ahead of Richard, in the Atlanta race to take a two-point lead into the final race.

The title duel was being portrayed as a western-style shoot-out by Ontario Motor Speedway publicists, and even Waltrip described it as a classic confrontation. "Richard has the experience, he's been on top, and he's won the title six times already. My team has been in business only a third as long as the Pettys and here we are, the underdog, challenging him for the title."

I had never seen a team in such a tight championship battle as calm and confident as the Petty bunch. I had a long talk with Maurice during dinner two nights before the race, and he explained the history of the engine that he had picked for Richard to use. Maurice knew it was durable enough to go the distance and strong enough for Richard to run up front.

Richard never showed any signs of emotion. If there were any concerns, they were well hidden behind his bright smile. But I knew how much he wanted to win this title – and it was more than he was willing to show.

"I've already got six of them, and this would be just another notch beside my name," he told me.

But wouldn't it be special to come back and win the championship after failing to win a single race the previous season?

"It would be very satisfying. But I never felt like I had to come back with another good year to prove anything. I never had any doubts about myself."

Richard played his strategy perfectly, right up until the time for the drivers to crawl into their cars and crank the engines.

Waltrip entered the room where the pre-race drivers meeting was being held and picked out a place that was not very crowded to sit. A few minutes later, Richard entered, looked around the room and picked out his seat – right beside Waltrip. He never stopped grinning the whole time.

Richard had promised that he wanted to win the race as much as he did the title and would be running hard to do it. Most of us in the media thought that was more of the propaganda that he was tossing Waltrip's way.

But he was as good as his word once the race began. When it was over, and he had beaten Waltrip for the championship by an 11-point margin, he seemed genuinely disappointed that he had not won the race, too.

Richard finished fifth, at the tail-end of the lead draft, while Waltrip finished a lap down.

I thought it odd that Richard showed very little emotion during post-race ceremonies.

"It is just hard for me to feel too good, running as hard as I did all day and winding up fifth," he said. "If I had won the championship and the race, I imagine I would be sky-high."

Dale Inman was just as low-keyed as his cousin. "Hey, the Redskins won," he told Richard when Richard brought the car back to the garage after the race.

"I thought Dale was going to congratulate me

Richard "guns down" Darrell Waltrip for his seventh Winston Cup title in 1979. This gag shot was taken before the final race of the season in Ontario, Calif.

on the championship, but that was the first thing he said," Richard related later.

Other drivers seemed more impressed by Richard's seventh championship than his own team. "Richard charged from start to the finish, and that is how championships are supposed to be won," said Cale Yarborough, who had won the previous three titles.

Some were surprised that Richard had raced so hard with the title on the line.

They shouldn't have been. It was the way Richard had won his six previous championships, too.

Waltrip received an expensive education in his title run against The King, but the experience paid off as he won three championships during the 1980s. And when Richard began his final season in 1992, Waltrip was among his biggest fans.

"I am going to miss Richard," Waltrip said. "He taught me a lot. He was hard on me, and at one time or another he was my biggest critic, as far as my attitude and how I drove and those type of things.

"Now, we are best friends, and I realize most of the things he was trying to tell me were true. I certainly respect him a lot more now than when I was getting started. Richard is a great man. I don't have many autographs or souvenirs, but I am going to have his."

He also had the distinction of being the last victim of a championship run by The King.

CAUGHT CHEATIN'

Stock car fans driving long distances to attend races at Charlotte Motor Speedway frequently schedule a stop at Petty Enterprises on their way back home. The Petty museum and garages in Level Cross are only a short distance from where Interstate Highways 40 & 85 intersect in Greensboro.

So even under normal circumstances, the large group of fans waiting outside Richard's shop on that bleak, gray Monday morning of October 11, 1983, was not unusual.

Circumstances were far from normal, however, and that was the reason I had arrived shortly after nine o'clock to join the fans waiting for Petty Enterprises to open.

On the door of the visitors' center was a hand-scrawled sign that said, "Sorry, We Are Closed."

No one knew when the center would open. The fans peered through the wire fence surrounding the compound in hopes of catching a glimpse of The King, the man they worshipped.

Richard was in his office, across the compound, in a series of long meetings. On other Monday mornings, he might have stepped outside to chat and sign autographs. This day he didn't.

I waited, along with sad-faced fans who were still in shock about what they had heard or read in the morning newspapers about Richard's victory the day before at Charlotte Motor Speedway.

Hours after Richard had driven under the checkered flag to put the 198th victory of his career in the record books, NASCAR officials announced that he had won the race with illegal tires and engine.

The King, for the first time in his life, had been caught cheating and, as one of the fans waiting outside the compound, had told me, "It is like accusing God of sinning."

The visitor center finally opened and within two hours more than a hundred Petty fans, dressed in Petty hats and jackets, were inside looking at the trophies. They moved slowly and talked in whispers.

> **F**or the first time in his career, Richard did not want to face reporters because he simply did not know how to explain the embarrassing mess.

"It is like a funeral in there," one fan told me. "It is just like someone died. Everyone is so upset."

Most fans simply refused to believe the accusations were true. There had to be some mistake, some explanation, they insisted.

But, yes, it was true. So undeniably true.

After Richard parked his car in Victory Lane, crew chief Larry Pollard stuck his head in the window and told him that on the last pit stop he had put left side tires on the right side of the car, which was against NASCAR rules. The left sides are softer and allow the car to get better traction in the turns to go faster.

What Pollard and Richard did not know at the time was that Maurice Petty, sick of his brother getting outrun by other cheaters on the circuit, had installed an over-sized engine for Richard to use in the race.

Richard, who had run fifth or sixth most of the afternoon behind swift leader Darrell Waltrip, had no idea how fast his car would go with the illegal tires until he blasted out of the final pit stop and began rapidly gaining ground on the front-runners.

Maybe Richard suspected something. Maybe he didn't. The crew had been adjusting the chassis on the car most of the day, and each time it seemed to get a little better. Now it was a whole lot better.

There was no reason for those of us in the press box to suspect anything was amiss. Over the years I had seen the Petty crew work with different combinations during a race and get it right for the stretch run. The only thing that did seem strange was how Waltrip seemed to allow Richard to make the pass for the lead when he caught him in the Number 2 turn.

Richard told me later that he did not understand that either.

Other than that, those of us in the press box saw it as just another win to move Richard closer to his 200th victory.

Lynda Petty, though, could tell something was not right as soon as Richard crawled out of the car in Victory Lane. Richard was smiling, as he always did – win or lose, but Lynda noticed that he seemed uptight.

The first indication reporters received that something might be wrong was that NASCAR inspectors seemed to be taking forever to clear Richard's car following the victory.

Then, during the end of Richard's press conference, NASCAR president Bill France, Jr., motioned for Richard to join him in another room. Richard twitched his shoulder, gave a blank expression and followed France to one of the nearby suites.

As France was telling Richard that the inspectors had found the illegal tires, he got another phone call. Now they had found Maurice's big engine, too. The engine was 24 cubic inches larger than the 358 cubic inches allowed by the rules.

Richard, who had expected NASCAR to discover the tires, was completely shocked. He could offer no defense, and he told France that he was willing to accept whatever penalty was warranted.

Four hours after the fans had left the speedway with no idea of what was happening, NASCAR announced that Richard would be allowed to keep the victory but was being fined a record $35,000 and 104 championship points.

Richard, who had returned to the garage after learning of the large engine violation, did not return to the press box. For the first time in his career, he did not want to face reporters because he simply did not know how to explain the embarrassing mess.

The immediate reaction from reporters and other competitors was that the penalty was not strong enough. Most, without talking to Richard, believed he did not deserve the victory and probably would not accept it.

Junior Johnson, who owned the car Waltrip drove to a second-place finish, felt, of course, that Richard should refuse the win. "If Richard did wrong, and he knows he did wrong, he should be man enough to not accept it," Johnson said when we called him from the press box.

Waltrip was in a tight battle with Bobby Allison for the Winston Cup championship. He said he wasn't angry with Petty, but he thought he should have the victory and the points that went with it.

Having followed Richard's career for more than two decades, I had mixed emotions as I drove away from the speedway to find a motel room near Level Cross. I had never known Richard to outright lie, so if he said he did not approve, or even know about the cheating, I would believe him. But I could not understand why he would want to tarnish his record by accepting a victory he knew had been won with illegal equipment.

That was the question that I kept asking myself while I waited the next day for Richard to clear out his morning appointments. Finally, about noon, I and a couple of other reporters were invited into Richard's office, which is decorated with memorabilia from his racing career.

Sitting behind his huge desk, Richard smiled weakly and asked, "What's happening, guys?"

"That is what we'd like to know," I replied.

Richard nodded, leaned back in his chair, and proceeded to relate all that he had learned about the dark deeds committed the day before by his brother and crewmen.

He confirmed that he did not know anything about the illegal tires or illegal engine until they were discovered separately by NASCAR inspectors. "I didn't come back to the press box after I found out because I was not man enough to face you. I didn't know what to tell you at the time."

Pollard told Richard he had put the illegal left side tires on the right side hoping to gain only two or three positions and had no idea they would improve the car enough for Richard to win the race.

Richard was upset that Pollard would do such a thing without him knowing about it. He was just as miffed at Maurice, who left the Petty compound early that Monday and was not around to answer questions.

Maurice later told me that he knew other teams were using over-sized engines, and that was the reason he put the engine in the car. He didn't tell Richard because he did not think Richard would approve it.

Some believed both Pollard and Maurice were taking the rap to protect Richard. But the facts did not bear out such a contention.

"I am not stupid," Richard reminded. "If I

know I have a big engine and the wrong tires, I am going to finish second or third. That way, no one inspects my car. Only a fool would take an engine too big and tires not legal to Victory Lane, knowing he is going to get caught."

Finally, I asked Richard if he was going to keep the victory.

He said his initial gut feeling was to tell NASCAR he did not want he victory because the evidence was there and it would be the first time in his life he had accepted something he might not deserve.

But he was not going to do that.

"If I don't get the victory, who gets it?" he asked. "And, how would anyone know for sure that car was legal?"

It was a good question, of course. The Johnson crew had loaded up Waltrip's car quickly and was one of the first teams to leave the track. Too, Richard was still puzzled by how easily he had passed Waltrip for the lead.

"It just wasn't like Darrell not to race me for the lead," he said. "I don't want to speculate, but it looks a little devious."

Richard also knew he had driven as hard as he could most of the race, and even with the whopper engine that Maurice had built for him, he was running only fifth until the illegal tires were bolted on during the last pit stop.

"I don't understand that," Richard said. "Or maybe I do."

There had been season-long speculation that several teams were using big engines, and Johnson admitted he was virtually positive that at least four other teams had won races that season with illegal engines.

If Johnson knew this, as he said, it would figure that he, like Maurice, had gotten fed up and built one of his own. No one could have blamed him.

Richard did not smile much during our talk, and it was apparent he did not have much sleep the night before. I asked if this was his worst moment in racing, and he frowned.

"Really, I have never faced anything like this before, and it is a situation I never thought I would be in," he said.

I told him some of the fans outside were saying they hoped he would not accept the victory. Richard understood their feelings, but he didn't feel there was anything else he could do. NASCAR already had declared the victory official.

"If this had been my 200th victory, I would have tried to give it back as soon as I learned things were not right," Richard told me. "I won't be satisfied until I get the 201st victory, so there will not be any question about it."

Richard heard a few boos at the remaining races that season.

In later years, as it became increasingly doubtful that there would be a 201st victory, the controversy surrounding the tainted 198th win was forgotten and seldom mentioned.

I did talk several times with Maurice about the reason he built the big engine. He never once expressed any regrets and said he was glad he had done it. He said it was the only way that he could force NASCAR's hand in cracking down on the cheating so prevalent that season.

The Charlotte incident did just that, too.

Embarrassed as much as Richard, NASCAR

adopted stronger penalties that included manda-
tory suspensions, and the dark era of monster
engines screeched to a quick close.

In retrospect, I was glad Richard withstood
the pressures to give up the victory – and not
because he may not have won 200 without it.

What we don't know, and never will, is how
many victories Richard himself was cheated out
of by others using oversized engines before
Maurice got fed up and built one of his own.

PETTY ENTERPRISES

I was grazing my way down a long table of appetizers at one of the social functions during race week at North Carolina Motor Speedway when I was intercepted by Maurice Petty. Right away, I figured out he had more than meatballs and chicken wings on his mind.

"I am going to kick your butt," Maurice informed me.

I had known, respected, and liked Maurice and his family for several years. I smiled, thinking it was a joke.

Maurice did not smile back, and I realized my butt might be in serious trouble.

Dale Earnhardt once told me that one of the golden rules in racing was not to get Maurice angry at you. It seemed pretty evident that somehow I had managed to do just that.

"Well, Maurice, if you are going to kick my butt, there isn't a thing I can do about it," I said. "But I'd like to know what the problem is."

"That story you wrote. It embarrassed me and my entire family."

"Huh, that story?"

There were reports that Richard was exploring opportunities to leave Petty Enterprises to drive for someone else.

"Yeah, that story."

"Oh, you mean *that* story," I said, finally recalling one that I thought was an objective look at the Petty family racing situation near the end of the 1981 season.

Maurice described the story in terms other than "objective."

Let me explain that 1981 was not a good year for Petty Enterprises, even though it began with Richard winning his seventh Daytona 500.

Several days after the Daytona victory, Dale Inman resigned from Petty Enterprises to become Dale Earnhardt's team manager.

Richard won only two more races that season and had his worst finish, eighth, in the Winston Cup championship standings.

The frustrations were expressed vividly by Lynda Petty in the November race at Atlanta after seeing Richard in the lead pack one minute and rolling slowly back to the garage, with a blown engine, the next.

"It is awful," she said. "Just awful. Especially when luck goes against you. It just seems to keep on and on. We can't get it turned around. Everyone is trying so hard, but it isn't showing."

Kyle was in his second year as the Number 2 driver for the family team. He wasn't having as much luck as his father.

There were reports that Richard was exploring opportunities to leave Petty Enterprises to drive for someone else. That way, he would have someone else paying his bills and salary and Kyle would be the only expense for Petty Enterprises.

On top of all that came a North Carolina magazine that printed an article alleging Richard and Maurice were in a long, bitter feud and not speaking to each other.

All of the above, with due credits, were discussed in my story which ran under a headline written by an editor that read: "Good Times Fade for Racing's First Family."

I like to think that the good people of the Pettys' small town in their own sweet way over-reacted to the story and made it worse than it was.

People were stopping Maurice and his wife on the streets, offering their sympathy, and a preacher in one of the local churches said a public prayer for them. While it doesn't say much for the story, it does say a lot about the deep feelings the town had for the Pettys.

"Do you have a brother?" Maurice asked me.

"I do."

"You ever have any arguments with him?"

"A few, yes."

"Do you love your brother?"

"Yeah, sure."

"Well," Maurice said, "my brother and I have not always agreed on everything, either. But I still love my brother."

It was a matter of record that Richard held similar feelings for Maurice, whom he several times described as being "the most courageous" member of the family.

I soon understood why Maurice was so upset. I assured him that I had not meant to embarrass him, his family, or Richard's family, by the story I had written.

We ended the conversation with both my butt and our friendship still intact.

The only other time I remember Maurice getting hold of me was a couple of years later when I unintentionally walked past him in the garage at Daytona International Speedway.

I felt someone grab my arm. I turned to see Maurice faking a glare at me. "Don't ever walk by me again without saying hello," he said, and broke into a big laugh.

I think that was in 1984, the year both Richard and Maurice quit working at Petty Enterprises and left the family business for Kyle to operate. Richard left to drive for a new team formed by West Coast millionaire Mike Curb, and Maurice went into a brief period of semi-retirement.

Petty Enterprises, once the grand castle of stock car racing's greatest team, was only a shell when I visited it before the start of the 1984 season. I was struck with the thought that if buildings could cry, the compound of engine rooms and garages might well be under water.

Instead of the 25 or so mechanics who once built the best cars on the circuit, there were only a dozen or so, and most were like Kyle, just starting their careers.

"We used to have a lot of people who could do only one job each. Now we have fewer people who can do two or three jobs," Kyle told me.

Kyle explained that his father's departure was strictly business. "We found out we couldn't both run out of here. Look at the record, and you see that. Daddy quit winning regularly when we tried to run two teams. My effort pulled Daddy's car down, and it didn't help my car, either."

There did not seem any doubt that Kyle was in charge, as the neighborhood dog already had learned. The new boss booted him out of the compound.

"So I kick dogs," Kyle said jokingly. "Sometimes you have to be ruthless in this business."

Sometime between that January day and early August, Kyle learned just how unpleasant the real world business could be. He was told when Richard and Maurice moved out that he was in charge of Petty Enterprises. It wasn't ever that way, however. He was only a figurehead, and the key decisions were still being made by the owners, Richard, Maurice, and Lee.

"I can't fault them. I can't say anything bad against them," Kyle told me during a long talk we had one afternoon at the Talladega Superspeedway. "The deal is it is their company. You know what I mean? If I had a company and had run it for thirty years or so, I would be real leery of turning it over to someone else to run, too.

"That is just the way it is. But I think one of the things that has happened is racing has passed Petty Enterprises by. When I came along, everything was supposed to be great and a bed of roses. Somewhere down the line I fell into a patch of thorns."

Kyle already had decided that he would leave the family team, too, at the end of the season to drive for the Wood Brothers, once Petty Enterprises' strongest rival on the superspeedways.

"Sometimes it is better to close the doors on a place and move on," Kyle said. "It might be that time, and they can turn Petty Enterprises into a museum."

Kyle left at the end of the season with Richard's blessings and understanding. "He's got to look out for himself and not worry about Petty Enterprises," Richard said.

When the 1985 season began, Maurice came back and opened the doors for another racing season. But he was fighting an almost impossible battle. He took an unsponsored pearly-white Ford Thunderbird to the Daytona 500 for Dick Brooks to drive.

Maurice recognized the odds were stacked high against him, but it was worth the effort, he thought. "Hey, if this doesn't work out, I ain't going to have to look up to anybody," he said.

The Ford was competitive, but after only a few races Maurice had to shut the doors again at Petty Enterprises after failing to get sponsorship to run the remainder of the schedule.

Meanwhile, Richard was going through a winless season in 1985 with the Curb team. There were many problems that Richard might have solved if he had been running the team. But they were out of his control as driver.

It was a new experience for Richard, and he

didn't like it. He didn't complain publicly, but he told me in August, "I can only blame myself for getting into this situation, and it's up to me to get out of it."

He already had decided that after finishing the year with the Curb team he was going back to the family team, reopen the doors, and try to rebuild it to where it was during his glory days.

Richard already had talked to Dale Inman about how great it would be to go back to the old place and be together again on the same team. When Dale, who had guided young Terry Labonte to the Winston Cup title in 1984, learned that Richard was serious, he became excited, too.

Dale got an early release from Labonte's team in September and began getting the old place ready for The King's return in 1986. If Richard was starting over, it was only fitting that Dale be there, too.

Dale was in Richard's pit when he began his career at Columbia Speedway in 1958, and it seemed natural for him to return to Petty Enterprises when Richard began the final phase of his driving career.

Dale says he really began going to races with the Pettys in the early 1950s but didn't collect his first paycheck until 1963. "I just had that kind of love for it," he says.

"It seems Richard and I have been together ever since he learned to walk and I learned to walk. I am not saying we were always that close, but we were always together. We went to the same swimming hole and got poison oak all over us. We would jump in a creek called Pole Cat Creek. It was always cold, and you were liable to see a water moccasin slide in there with you."

They raced bicycles together, and when they got old enough, they banged a few fenders together. "We did a lot of things we shouldn't have done, and we got our share of speeding tickets," Dale said.

They played football together at Randleman High School. Dale was a 145-pound halfback and Richard was a 215-pound tackle. "Now, I weigh a ton and Richard weighs about 170 pounds," Dale laughed as he took a break from preparing The King's car for its final Daytona 500 in 1992.

Dale did not want to get too emotional about Richard's farewell season, and he was the one in charge of making sure that Richard remained focused on racing during a season when distractions were everywhere. Still, when Richard received a standing ovation from other drivers before the Daytona 500, Dale had to brush a few tears from his eyes.

There were lots of good times, victories and championships to remember.

There was a future, too.

Richard was still going be there after the '92 season as the car owner. Dale would be there, too, doing what he could to bring Petty Enterprises back to the front of the pack.

Richard just barely reaches the finish line ahead of Cale Yarborough to begin a race-ending caution period to win the 1984 Firecracker 400 at Daytona. It was Richard's 200th career victory.

WINNING 200

I have written about sports heroes for more than three decades while enjoying friendships with many of them.

Yet, I have an autographed picture of only one of those sports celebrities on a wall in my home.

It is a poster that STP released after Richard Petty's 200th career victory at Daytona International Speed-way in the 1984 Firecracker 400.

It is a color picture of The King, smiling under his cowboy hat, and the cars of Richard and Cale Yarborough speeding to the finish line to begin a race-ending caution period.

Hardly a day slips by that I do not pause, stare at that picture and still find myself amazed at how narrow the margin was in what would become the final jewel in the The King's crown.

None of us at the time, and certainly not Richard, had any idea that one of the grander moments in racing history also would mark a sad turning point in the career of the the greatest winner the sport had ever known.

As much as Richard wanted to get Number 200 out of the way at Charlotte, it turned out that there was an even better stage for him to give the most celebrated performance of his jeweled career.

Richard had come back from his second winless season in 1982, to win races at Rockingham, Talladega, and Charlotte in 1983, leaving him only three victories short of 200.

Now, in 1984 and 46 years old, Richard was embarking on a brand new adventure as the national motorsports media prepared to chart his quest for No. 200. Richard had left the family team to his son, Kyle, and had gone down the road to drive for a new team owned by West Coast politician and recording producer Mike Curb.

The deal came together only a few weeks before the start of the season, and there seemed to be problems on top of problems, so it was not surprising that Richard got off to a slow start.

The season was eight races old when I visited with Richard at the Talladega Superspeedway. We talked about how the new job was shaping up and his feelings about where he was in his career.

Richard had won only $42,495 for his new

team, while Darrell Waltrip had collected $224,735, and Cale Yarborough, driving in only four major events, had won $181,365. But Richard was not discouraged.

He told me he was satisfied with his career, and that he did not feel pressure to become a quick winner with his new team.

"I don't have to prove nothing to nobody. If I never run another race, if I never finish another race, or if I never win another race, I don't feel like there is anything left for me to prove.

"I never felt when we put this team together I had anything to prove. The only one I have got to satisfy is myself. If I go out and do a good job, or feel like I have done a good job, I am at peace with myself. And as long as I am at peace with myself, I am all right."

Still, he admitted, he wanted to get on to the next victory if only to put behind the tainted victory at Charlotte the previous season. "I'd like to win four or five times this season so I can go on and get over the hump, get away from the 200 completely, and forget about it," he said. "That way, I would not only be off it, but completely away from it and all of that other stuff would definitely be in the past."

Richard knew that once he won Number 200 no one would worry about him winning 201, or whatever else followed. "There won't be no next after that. You know what I mean? You just go on and do it then without all of this stuff going on around you."

Richard had won only three races in the last two seasons, and he understood he would never dominate the circuit as he once did, but I found him still comfortable with his title as The King.

"If some cat comes along and wins eight or ten races a year on different size tracks, you can say he is the one you got to beat," Richard explained. "But someone that wins three or four races a year, he is not the one to beat because there are still others winning a lot of races, too."

Richard said people still considered him The King because nobody else had come along and done as much as he had. "None of them have been able to knock me off the deals I did five years ago, ten years ago, or twenty years ago. See what I mean? No one has been able to shoulder the sport by himself.

"I don't think I could ever dominate again like I done in the past. Maybe I am not that pushy now. Not that I've had my ride in the sunset, but I can see it is going downhill. I can still have some good years, still win some races and still be a dominant figure. But I don't think there will be a situation where I win thirteen, fifteen, or twenty-seven races in a season again."

Some recently-born experts were proclaiming that Richard couldn't dominate the way he did in previous decades because of so much more competition.

I knew better. So did Richard.

"When I used to dominate, it wasn't because I didn't have competition," Richard told me. "It was just that my team was so dadgum much better than the rest. You know what I mean?"

I did know what he meant, and it was only a couple of weeks later on the physically-tough Dover Downs International Speedway that Richard proved he still had the winning touch by putting career victory Number 199 into the record book.

Harry Gant dominated for most of the long, hot day until his Chevrolet coasted into the garage with a hole in the oil pan. Richard, who had been planning a down-the-stretch run at Harry, took control and won rather easily.

His crew, led by Buddy Parrott, hoisted a banner in the pits that read "199," just in case anyone had lost count.

It was Richard's first victory for a team other than Petty Enterprises, but even the wisest trivia buffs may have forgotten that he rode under the checkered flag on Petty Enterprises tires.

Richard, who had used up all of his fresh tires, borrowed the last six that were bolted on his car from his son, Kyle.

And, while it was Richard's first victory away from home, it was in an old Petty Enterprises car that Curb had purchased before the start of the season.

The "199" banner definitely was not Richard's idea. As was his custom, he seemed the least excited of all that he was only one victory away from Number 200.

"It feels like just another victory," Richard said after walking through a cheering mob to reach the press box on top of the front grandstands.

"But I guess if you would pick out my twenty-fifth victory, or thirtieth, it wouldn't seem nearly as important as this one right now. In fact, when I won my hundredth race, I don't think anyone made much noise about it. We just went on and won one-hundred-and-one, and so on."

There was no question that Richard wanted to win 200.

The reason, he told those of us in the press box that day at Dover, was so "You won't keep asking me about it, and I can go on racing, and people will know that I am not going to retire after I get the two-hundredth win in the books."

But only one step away from Number 200, Richard began getting even more attention. Everyone kept asking when he was going to win it, and if he would retire once he did. The motorsports world was focusing on Richard with the same intensity and anticipation with which baseball enthusiasts had followed Hank Aaron's pursuit of Babe Ruth's home run record.

The big difference was that Richard wasn't chasing anyone else. The only record he could break was his own.

The next race was at Charlotte, and that is where Richard most wanted to win his 200th race.

It seemed an appropriate location since Richard had won his first Winston Cup race on a Charlotte dirt track that preceded the one-and-half-mile oval that was built in 1960.

There were other reasons, too. The next race was scheduled for Riverside, Calif., where racing was not nearly as big as it was in the Carolinas. "I consider Charlotte my home track, and it would mean much more to me to win it here," Richard said.

Most of all, Richard wanted to win at Charlotte just to put all the hoopla behind him. "I like talking to you, but I hate to keep answering same questions over and over," he said.

Rivals who had not considered Richard a serious contender on the circuit only a few weeks earlier now were picking him as the favorite at Charlotte.

"The track is awfully slick, and if anyone hits the right combination, he could take off from everyone," veteran crew chief Harry Hyde said. "I'd say if anyone finds that combination, it will be Richard. He likes to run a soft setup and that works best on a slick tick. He is one of a few drivers who will drive a car that rolls and wallows through the turns on such a setup."

Richard wanted to win at Charlotte, and others were expecting him to do so. But when he awoke Sunday morning in his Level Cross home, Richard knew that Number 200 would come some other time, some other track.

Concession stands were doing a booming business selling "200" caps and T-shirts, but The King could have told fans to save their money.

The engine quit in the red and blue Pontiac after only 216 laps, just past the halfway mark, and Richard was not surprised.

"Have you ever had a premonition?" he asked.

"Well, I didn't know exactly what was going to happen, but I knew when I woke up this morning I was not going to win this race. I didn't have a good night, and this is probably one of the most depressing days I've ever had."

As much as Richard had wanted to get Number 200 out of the way at Charlotte, it turned out that there was an even better stage for him to give the most celebrated performance of his jeweled career.

Richard had never done anything in a conventional manner, so why should we have expected differently when he finally gave the motorsports world the victory he was so anxiously awaiting?

President Ronald Reagan, who had given the command to start the 1984 Daytona 500 from the Oval Office, agreed to give the starting order for the Firecracker 400 at Daytona from closer range.

The president gave the command from Air Force One as it was on its way to Daytona, where Mr. Reagan would become the first president to watch a stock car race at the track while in office. Race fans saw the huge Air Force One make its approach and seemingly aim for the backstretch of the Daytona track. But it touched down just beyond the backstretch wall at the adjacent Daytona airport.

The president was driven to the speedway to watch the final half of the race, and took time to join Motor Racing Network announcer Ned Jarrett in the radio booth. A one-time baseball announcer, Reagan accepted Jarrett's invitation to call a few laps of the race.

How did he do?

Let's just say he was a better president than he was announcer. "Here they come, there they go," Mr. Reagan informed MRN listeners.

Fortunately, the president was not still at the microphone when the race came down to the final three laps, with Cale Yarborough locked in a tight draft behind Richard, who was leading.

It was apparent that Yarborough, a master of the slingshot move by which a car slips out of the draft of the lead car and picks up extra horsepower to make a pass, was waiting until the final lap to play his strategy.

But his hand was forced prematurely when Doug Heveron wrecked in the first turn to bring out a caution flag. Both Richard and Cale realized the race to the caution flag would decide the victory, since there was not enough time to clear the track in the final two laps to finish under the green flag.

Cale made his move in the third turn, whipping out of the draft, to slingshot into the lead. But the quick burst of speed also carried Cale's Chevrolet to the top of the track, giving Richard the chance to drop his Pontiac low and pull even in the fourth turn.

The two cars bumped as both drivers aimed for the fast lane. Richard refused to yield an inch, and he used a final grinding bump to get the momentum he needed to reach the checkered flag only a couple of feet ahead of Cale.

The victory fit for a King also was admired by a president.

"I couldn't believe you two were bumping each other like that at two-hundred miles per hour," Richard said the president told him.

For both Richard and Cale it was just hard racing.

Richard made his visit to Victory Lane and was off to be congratulated by the president in a special bullet-proof VIP box. Later, both Richard and the president joined a Fourth of July picnic in the garage area.

Richard knew his 200th victory would have grabbed headlines on the sports page no matter where it came, or who was watching. But with President Reagan in attendance, it got front-page coverage and was carried by the networks on their prime time news programs.

Richard considered the extra publicity that the president helped to generate as a payback of sorts, since he had been on the campaign trail for

him. "He will get my name in some places that I couldn't, but then I've gotten his name into some places that he couldn't," The King reminded.

President Reagan seemed to enjoy himself at the race and the picnic. "It is such courage and skill by these drivers and mechanics that have made stock car racing a major American sport," he said. "If Patrick Henry was alive today, I am sure he would be a stock car driver, too."

If I could have got close enough to the president, I would have told him that if Richard Petty had been alive in 1776, we'd probably see his name on the Declaration of Independence, too.

Faces, Family and Friends

1963

1964

1966

1967

1968

1969

Faces, Family and Friends

1980

1992, just before final race at Daytona

Faces, Family and Friends

Richard celebrates in victory lane with his young daughters.

Richard and Kyle talk racing at Martinsville Speedway in Virginia.

Faces, Family and Friends

Present and future generations: At left, Richard's wife, Lynda, listens during a ceremony honoring Richard prior to the start of the 1992 Daytona 500. Above, Richard gives some racing advice to his granddaughter, Montgomery Lee Petty, at the starting line of the 1990 Pepsi Junior 400.

Faces, Family and Friends

National motorsports media representatives get a look at Richard's new cars during the 1990 pre-season tour.

Faces, Family and Friends

Richard looks at portraits of the late Bobby and Billy Myers after becoming the first three-time winner of the Myers Brothers Award for outstanding contributions to stock car racing.

Faces, Family and Friends

"The Richard Petty Achievement Award" will be presented annually by STP. The announcement came during pre-race ceremonies honoring Richard at the 1992 Daytona 500.

Richard receives a checkered flag signed by other drivers prior to the start of his final Daytona 500 in 1992.

Faces, Family and Friends

Going out in style: Richard waves to fans during a pre-race lap prior to the start of the 1992 Daytona 500.

WINNING ISN'T EVERYTHING

Buck Baker was far down the backside of the mountain top he once occupied in stock car racing when he came to Hampton, Va., a day early to beat the publicity drums for a minor league race in which he would be competing.

I don't remember the exact year, probably around 1970, but I'll never forget the lesson I learned that night.

Buck and I enjoyed a nice dinner at the motel where he was staying and headed back to his room for a few drinks. There is not a better story teller anywhere than Buck, although his son, Buddy, comes pretty close, and I never pass up an opportunity to hear his humorous stories.

Hours ticked by like minutes as Buck reminisced about the days when he raced against men such as Little Joe Weatherly, Curtis Turner, Fireball Roberts, and Lee Petty. The sun was beginning to peek over the Chesapeake Bay when I realized that it was time for me to head for home so that Buck, who was to race that day, could get some rest.

Life outside of victory lane was a new and frequently disappointing experience for the Pettys, but no one could have handled it better or with more class.

Before I left, though, I asked Buck to explain something that was puzzling me. During his glory days, Buck was among the best and most successful drivers in the sport. He was the first driver to win back-to-back NASCAR championships in 1956-57 and the first driver to win three Southern 500 races at Darlington. His last Darlington win was in 1964, and it provided him the perfect opportunity to walk away while still a champion.

"Why are you still out here racing?" I asked. "Do you ever wish that you had quit after that last Southern 500 victory?"

Buck smiled, shook his head and motioned for me to sit down.

"Let me explain something to you," he began. "I did not start racing because I wanted to win championships and races and be able to say I left while on top of the sport. I could have done that when I won my first Southern 500 in 1954 or my first championship. I started racing because it was fun, something I wanted to do.

"I am racing because it is still fun and something I want to do. I have never regretted quitting earlier just so someone could say that I went out on top. If I had done that, I would have missed a lot of fun. Sure, I know this isn't the big-time. But it is still racing, and I am having a ball."

Because of the lesson I learned that night, I never was one of those who thought that Richard Petty would – or should – retire after winning his 200th race in 1984. I knew Richard did not begin racing with the intention of winning seven national championships and 200 races. So it did not make sense that simply putting those numbers in the record books would be reason enough for him to quit.

Richard loved racing, and not just when he was winning.

I once asked Richard what he would have done had he not got into racing. He thought for a few moments and shrugged. "I have been in racing, helping Daddy at first, just about all my life," he said. "I really never thought about doing anything else."

The only hint as to what he might have done if he hadn't been racing came in the early 1970s, when he was angry about one of NASCAR's many politically motivated rule changes that left his car at a disadvantage.

"I might just quit racing," Richard said. "I have won enough money that I don't ever have to race again if I don't want to."

"But Richard," I said. "If you didn't race, what would you do?"

"Oh, I don't know. Maybe go farming," he said.

Richard did enjoy climbing on a tractor and rumbling over the fields during the off-weekends. But nothing ever could have taken the place of crawling into a race car.

The only person who could completely appreciate how much Richard loved to race is his wife, Lynda. If she had not understood, she would not have survived being Mrs. Richard Petty.

I've heard Richard jokingly say he told Lynda before they were married that racing was Number 1 in his life, and if she tried real hard that she could be Number 2.

Richard was already racing, and Lynda was still in Randleman High School when they began dating. One day, out of the blue, Richard told Lynda that if they were going to get married they had better do it soon or else he would not have time to be fooling with a thing like that.

"He told me that when things got going if we didn't do it then, he might not ever get married," Lynda recalls. "Knowing him, that didn't surprise me, because that's how he does things – like, bam! I knew if I was going to be a part of Richard Petty's life, that it had to be right then."

Without telling anyone, they drove to Chesterfield, S.C., and signed for a license. The next night they went back and got married.

"It cost us $24, and when we started back home Richard told me he was going to give me a wedding present," Lynda says. "It was a hundred dollar bill. I had never seen one of those before in my life."

Lynda knew Richard was serious when he said that racing was his life. She made it her way of life, too, standing by her man during the best times, as well as the not-so-good times.

"We had absolutely zero, except each other, when we started out," Lynda says. "We lived with Richard's mother and daddy for a year, and life was really simple. Along came Kyle and Sharon, and we built a house out beside his parents' house, and life was still fairly simple.

"We just went to the races. He raced, and we got in the payoff line, and we went home. We bought groceries and cooked them. We slept, got up, and went to the next race. All the time, racing was growing and changing. But it is like when you are in the middle of something, you don't see it changing. It is just like children. All at once you look around and say, 'Hey, they are grown. Where have all the years gone?' "

Lynda began noticing the changes when the circuit left the smaller tracks and roared onto the big, paved superspeedways. "We didn't go to Greenville-Pickens any more. We didn't go to Wilson. We didn't go to Columbia," Lynda says.

There were other changes, too. Sponsorship advertisements began showing up on the sides of race cars, for instance. "I can show you pictures of Richard's early race cars, and there was not a sticker on them, just 'Plymouth by Petty,' " Linda said. "We raced because we loved it. If Richard had to work on the car all night, me and the kids would bring food over and stay in the garage all night. We did what we had to do to get to the next race, and no one complained."

Those days were well in the past when Richard, accompanied by Dale Inman, went back to Petty Enterprises for the 1986 season. He had not won a race since getting Number 200 midway through the 1984 season, but he was brimming with determination and confidence that he could move back and things would be like they were in the good ol' days.

"We know we are going to win races," Richard told me. "We have done it before. A lot of them cats thinking they are going to win races have never done it."

But racing had taken another giant growing spell. Richard – being in the middle of it – didn't realize just how much things had changed in the couple of years he had been away from Petty Enterprises.

I guess it would be easy for some people to say that once Richard got Number 200 that he just eased off the throttle and coasted through the final years of his career. Nothing could be farther from the truth, however.

Richard wanted to win as much as he ever did, and his driving skills were still at a level high enough for him to win consistently. But Richard no longer had the top-flight organization and stability behind him that he had enjoyed during his triumphant years. I think he learned, too, that rebuilding Petty Enterprises was a bigger and more expensive task than he had envisioned, and demanded more time than he had to give.

Maybe if he could have been there in the garage night and day, as in the early years, things would have clicked a lot sooner. But while Richard still lived to race, racing was no longer his entire life. First this and then that kept pulling him away from the race car, and filling his head with many thoughts.

"Racing is as important as it's ever been to me, but the big difference is that there are a lot of other important things taking up space in my computer," Richard said, tapping his head.

"My life has gotten a lot bigger since those days when I didn't have anything else to do but race. There are so many more things for me to think about. My kids, my grandchildren, running a business, personal appearances, and everything else that is happening in my life."

Richard told me if he could take an entire year without having to do business engagements, appearances, and interviews that he could turn things around and resume winning races and championships.

We both knew that was impossible, because without doing the appearances and interviews there would be no sponsor and with no sponsor there would be no money with which to race. A car with just "Pontiac by Petty" on it would not get very far in racing during the 1980s.

As one winless season followed another in the final years of Richard's career as a driver, a few things did become increasingly clear to everyone. Richard didn't lose his love for racing when the winning stopped, and Lynda never regretted running off and marrying into a life of racing.

Life outside of victory lane was a new and frequently disappointing experience for the Pettys, but no one could have handled it better or with more class.

"Winning is not everything, and Richard is an example of that," Lynda said. "Even though we don't win, and even though we get beat week after week, we just can't complain because life has been so good to us. We will have those memories to draw on when we are a hundred years old."

As sweet as the memories were from the winning years, the best of all may have been saved for the last few seasons when Richard's immense popularity and status as "The King" remained rock-solid in defeat. Heroes of the new era complained about not having time to sign autographs and do interviews, but Lynda would smile as she watched Richard stand there and make the kids, and a lot of adults, happy with the flick of the pen.

Winning never was everything to Richard Petty.

It wasn't to The King's many fans either.

A RACE WITHOUT RICHARD

By watching and studying the best stock car drivers for more than three decades, I came to learn that a driver's greatest strengths sometimes can be his biggest weaknesses. I know, that sounds a little confusing.

But take Dale Earnhardt, the only driver other than Richard Petty to win more than three Winston Cup championships. His strong suit is his aggressive, hard-driving style. At other times, it has got him into trouble and cost him a few victories and at least one national championship.

I think one of Richard's strengths – just plain ol' hard-headed stubbornness and determination – was one of the reasons for his worst season as a driver.

I could tell 1989 was not going to be a good year for Richard when I walked through the Daytona garage area during SpeedWeek and saw Richard staring at his red and blue Pontiac as if he were contemplating murder.

Richard stood for the longest time, his cowboy hat pushed back on his head, hands on hips,

One of Richard's strengths – just plain 'ol hard-headed stubbornness and determination – was one of the reasons for his worst season as a driver.

and seemed to be staring a hole in the car. If looks could kill, the Pontiac would have been a goner. If Richard had had a gun, I believe he might have pumped Ol' 43 full of lead.

Finally, he shook his head in disgust and walked to the team truck, putting the too-slow Pontiac out of sight, if not out of mind.

"It is just so dadgum frustrating," Richard said after I had given him a couple of minutes to cool down. He took the wrapper off a cigar, stuck it in his mouth and leaned against the wall of a small office at the end of the truck.

"You keep trying to figure out what else you can do to make the car run faster, but nothing we try seems to work. Oh, yeah. There are a lot of arm-chair quarterbacks. Everyone knows what the problem is except the poor old coach and quarterback, who don't know nothing."

The man who had won seven Daytona 500s, who held the event record as its youngest winner (26 in 1964), who had won the 1973 race by five miles, was now facing the possibility that he might not even win a starting position for the biggest race of the season. His Pontiac just couldn't get up to speed against all the stronger Fords and Chevrolets.

Richard thought a big problem was the carburetor restricter plates NASCAR was requiring everyone to use at Daytona and Talladega to keeps speeds under 200 miles per hour. The plates slowed down the cars, all right, but they also took so much power out of the engines that drivers were mostly playing follow-the-leader.

The "slingshot," the high-speed drafting tactic that Richard discovered on the Daytona high banks in the early 1960s, was now a lost art. The cars didn't have enough power to make a clean pass without another car helping to push it through the wind.

Richard also was among a group of drivers handicapped when NASCAR dictated radical body changes to their cars only two weeks before they were to arrive in Daytona.

"When we tested during the winter we were as good as we have ever been with this car," Richard said. "Then NASCAR got us again. Everything we did and learned in the winter test was just a waste of time."

Richard had been the victim of NASCAR politics before, such as the times NASCAR outlawed the hemi engine, barred the SuperBird, and refused to give him any help in making his Dodge competitive during his first winless season in 1978.

"If I don't make this race, I might get me a pencil and pad and do one of them tell-all deals," Richard smiled. "But I don't know if there is enough paper in the world for me to tell it all."

I told Richard it seemed unbelievable that he would be left out of a Daytona 500 starting field.

"Well, I have never done anything believable in my life," he reminded. "I am not worried about it. You can speculate nine hundred ways and it all is just a waste of time."

Instead of being discouraged, Richard was more determined to solve his problems and get back to the fast groove. "Something like this just makes you madder and you work harder to get things squared away," he said.

That was why Richard made the 1989 Daytona 500, starting 34th and finishing a respectable 17th.

But more problems were waiting when the circuit finally got to Richmond International Raceway in late March for the Pontiac Excitement 400. The race was postponed for four weeks by inclement weather, which also delayed the first-round qualifying session another day.

Because of the weather, drivers got very little practice time before qualifying finally began on Saturday. Richard failed to reach a speed fast enough to win one of the 20 starting positions available in the first session.

The second-round of qualifying was scheduled for a couple of hours later. Richard seemed confident the car would be fast enough to make the field, but that changed when he crashed in final practice and didn't have time to get a backup car ready before the last round of qualifying.

Still, everyone felt certain there had to be some way for Richard to be included in the starting field. We all had seen NASCAR officials previously thumb through the rulebook and find an exception for "a rare instance."

This certainly seemed to qualify. Richard Petty had been in a record 513 consecutive Winston Cup races, and during the winning years Richmond was one of his favorite romping grounds. Thirteen of his 200 victories were in Richmond, including a seven-win streak during the early '70s.

In 1971, when NASCAR was juggling the rules again to keep Richard from winning so often, I saw him start from the rear of the field and, despite being penalized by a restricter plate, win by two laps.

NASCAR dictated that he use the plate and start last because his engine could not be fitted close enough to the front of the car. Richard figured the plate knocked out about fifty horsepower, but he still led 349 of the 500 laps.

That was during the good ol' days. In 1989, the worst of times, nothing was going right for King Richard.

After missing the final round of qualifying, Richard met with NASCAR officials while his mechanics continued to prepare the backup car for the race. The meeting took longer than it should have, and a couple of other reporters joined me in waiting for it to end.

Finally, the man who always had smiled through every disappointment imaginable emerged from the NASCAR trailer with a stone-cold expression on his frowning face. "I am going home, guys," Richard said. "They just told me I don't have a starting place in this race."

NASCAR was telling Richard Petty that he didn't have a place in this race? It seemed impossible.

I followed Richard back to his garage stall, where he broke the news to the mechanics working on his car. "Load it up and put everything on the truck," he ordered.

Richard had not missed a NASCAR race since Nov. 7, 1971, when he sat out an event at Macon, Ga., because the promoter was not willing to pay the drivers the same amount of show money as other promoters paid. Richard thought it would be unfair to the other promoters if he raced for someone else for a cheaper price. His streak of 513 consecutive races, some of which he started with a broken neck, broken ribs, or a busted shoulder, began the following week at Richmond, of all places.

Other drivers were as shocked by NASCAR's decision as everyone else. Rodney Combs was among those who offered to let Richard start his car so he could continue the streak. Richard refused.

I spoke privately to Richard briefly before he left the track. "Thirty years, a thousand races, and 500 straight starts don't mean a dadgum thing," he said bitterly. "When you make a living doing something and they don't let you try to make it, it is tough."

It was more than tough. It hurt, and it hurt bad.

"It had to be the worst hurt Richard ever had," Lynda Petty said. "It was like a death to load that car and drive out of that track and make that ride home. I cried all the way back."

There was once a day in NASCAR racing when promoters would not have dared run a race if Richard Petty was not in the field.

Joe Littlejohn, a pioneer promoter and member of racing's Hall of Fame, was one of them.

"If I had a race and Richard wasn't there, no one would have come to see it," Joe once told me.

Richmond promoter Paul Sawyer, who had known the Pettys since the '50s, wouldn't have started his race without Richard either, if it had been his decision.

But NASCAR was in charge, and circuit director Dick Beaty said he regretted very much that Richard did not make the field, but that rules were rules and everyone had to be treated the same.

If that had been NASCAR's history, fine.

But it wasn't.

We all could remember other days, for other drivers, when NASCAR twisted, bent, and rewrote its rules. As NASCAR president Bill France Jr., frequently reminded me, "None of our rules are written in stone."

But there would be no deviation this time. Not for Richard Petty, the man who had done more than anyone else to make stock car racing the popular sport it had become.

"I just can't believe NASCAR is not letting Richard in this race," Rusty Wallace said. "He ought to be here. I mean, he is The King. I hope when I win 200 races that I will get some respect."

I could not remember the last time I arrived at a speedway on race morning when Richard was not there. Even when he was hurt and couldn't drive, he was there to greet fans and sign autographs.

Some fans came not knowing Richard wouldn't be there and were sorely disappointed to discover that he wasn't. Thomas and Becky Bailey, longtime Petty followers from Fredericksburg, Va., said if they had known Richard was not going to race they would have stayed at home.

It seemed many fans did just that, too. For the first time in a long time the Richmond track failed to sell out for a Winston Cup race.

As I walked through the grandstands that morning, several fans asked me if I thought Richard would be so disgusted with the way NASCAR treated him that he would end his career. I didn't know what Richard was thinking, but I knew NASCAR would have been happy if Richard had retired. I was told this by a very high official.

Richard had scared everyone with his spectacular crash at Daytona in 1988, and a few months later the sport went through a nervous period that was created by Bobby Allison's terrifying and career-ending crash at Pocono, Pa. NASCAR officials, and a lot of others, did not want to see Richard go out that way.

"You would have thought not making the Richmond race would have been the one time that Richard threw in the towel," Lynda Petty says. "But it just made him more determined to go back and keep trying."

Richard failed to make the starting field for the next race, at North Wilkesboro, N.C., and missed a third race, at Bristol, Tenn., later in the season. When I talked to other drivers about the problems Richard was having, they would point to his race car, shake their heads, and say something just was not right. It did not look like any other Pontiac in the garage.

As I later learned from talking to Richard, the Pontiac was not like any other in the garage. The

Petty team was experimenting in hopes of getting an advantage that would put them at the front of the field again.

"That was how we got the edge back when I was winning races. We didn't do what everyone else was doing. But this time the stuff we tried just didn't work," Richard said.

I was reminded of another conversation I'd had with Richard about how racing had changed. In a long-gone era, the Pettys had won races by being smarter than other teams, and developing their own parts. But there were not many secrets in the sport any more, and all the good parts were available to everyone. "I'm not any smarter in buying parts than anyone else," Richard said.

In 1989, Richard was hard-headed enough to believe that maybe there were a few secrets left to discover. When he didn't find them that season, I think his head got a little softer. He reorganized his team, going in the direction of modern standards. He told me he was going to listen more closely to the bright, young mechanics he was hiring.

The improvement was apparent at the start of the 1990 season as Richard once again was competitive during SpeedWeek at Daytona. He had told me many times he would not consider retiring until he got Petty Enterprises headed back toward the top.

I didn't know it at the time, but he was going fast enough in 1990 that he could see that day coming.

RETIREMENT

Richard Petty says the first time anyone told him he should retire as a driver was after winning 27 races and his second national championship during the 1967 season. But I don't remember it ever being an issue, or anyone seriously questioning Richard about it.

The first time I discussed retirement with Richard was after the bad crash he had at Darlington in 1970. Richard had given no indication that he had lost any of his love for racing because of the accident, but it was bad enough that it could have given some people second thoughts.

Richard told me he always thought when he quit racing it would probably be when he got hurt and couldn't race any more. The Darlington wreck was not that bad, and he was just waiting for his left shoulder to mend so he could get back behind the steering wheel.

"I am just 32 years old and, really, feel that I've got several more years of racing ahead of me. If I were ready to quit, I certainly could use this as an excuse," he said. "But when I am ready

> **R**ichard told me he always thought when he quit racing it would probably be when he got hurt and couldn't race any more.

to quit, I might even use a hangnail as an excuse."

The first rumor that Richard was thinking about retiring got started late in the 1974 season. When I asked him about it before the Southern 500 at Darlington, he seemed more interested in learning how something like that got started than in denying it.

Probably, it was just wishful thinking by some competitors.

Indeed, when David Pearson heard the rumor, he jokingly tried to get me to encourage Richard to retire. "Just think of that big racing operation up in Randleman," Pearson said. "I think Richard ought to quit driving and stay up there to run the business. Why don't you go talk Richard into retiring? It would tickle me to death."

The first really hot rumor that Richard was going to retire, because of health reasons, came in 1975. Richard had begun to lose some of his hearing, and he frequently complained about headaches. He looked in good shape to me as he ran away from Pearson down the stretch to win the National 500 at Charlotte Motor Speedway in October.

When Richard came to the press box following the victory, the immediate questions concerned the retirement rumors, which already had been printed in one North Carolina newspaper. How bad was Richard's health?

"Truth is, I am about to die," Richard replied with a sad expression. Then he smiled and shook his head. "I do have problems and I hurt as much as anyone out here. But I have had about seven or eight physicals this year and the doctors can't find anything wrong."

Why so many physicals?

"It is because every time you do a commercial or endorse a product, they want to take out insurance on you. So, I have been getting a lot of physicals lately."

By not flatly denying the retirement rumors, Richard seemed to enjoy playing a cat-and-mouse game with the media. He would not say definitely that he was going to run the next race on the schedule, much less the entire next season.

Asked if he had signed a contract for the 1976 season with STP, his sponsor, Richard shook his head. "I don't think I have signed one for 1974 or 1975 yet," he answered. "All I know is that we are all set. Until STP calls up and says for me to send all the stickers back, I am still going."

Richard received a flood of letters and telegrams when the retirement rumors got into the newspapers. "I didn't know there were that many people who cared if I raced or not," he said. "But,

I am not committed to all those people. A few of them said, 'Hey, it is about time you quit,' and others said 'Hey, you can't quit now because I am betting on you.' "

Continuing health problems, the emergence of Kyle as a driver, and a decline in victories in following years continued to keep retirement rumors afloat. It was no secret, either, that Lynda Petty would like nothing better than to see her husband out of the race car. Those feelings she kept mostly to herself.

"We don't talk about it at home," Richard once told me. "Racing is what I want to do, and in my home the man makes the decisions. Lynda might think that I should quit, but she doesn't say it to me. I guess she knows if she did say it, I would just keep racing even longer. Some people might say I am stubborn, but I don't look at it that way. It is just that if I want to do something, I am going to do it, come hell or high water."

While Pearson was only joking about wanting Richard to retire in 1974, other drivers were passionately serious about it a few years later. Too many times they had seen him helped out the car, stretched out on the ground and given oxygen. "Richard Petty thinks he needs racing, but he doesn't," Cale Yarborough said in 1980. "I can't believe a man needs anything that is killing him."

Richard's reply: "Whether they like me or not, I think most drivers are genuinely concerned about me. You hate to see someone on top stay and stay and then get down to nothing. I guess sometimes in life you need to listen to what people are saying. I just ain't learned that yet."

If Richard had listened to what others were

saying at that time, he would not have won his final Daytona 500 in 1981, or his 200th race in 1984. He always figured that he would be the one to know when it was time for him to quit driving. He hoped one day to wake up with a realization that racing no longer was fun, and that would be it.

"If it ever comes to a point where I sit down for a few minutes to decide if I want to quit or not, I hope I will take that time to say 'That's it.' I am not saying I will. I just hope I will," he said.

When those initial thoughts of retirement finally entered his head, it took Richard considerably longer than a few minutes to say it.

It was after Richard's spectacular wreck in the 1988 Daytona 500. He was in a hospital room, aching all over, and Lynda walked into the room. So many times he had told her he would quit driving when it stopped being fun.

"Are we having fun?" she asked.

"Don't think so," Richard groaned.

"That was the beginning of it," Richard says. "I got to thinking about it, and for over a year it was in the back of my mind. I finally decided that was what I was going to do."

The decision was reached during the second half of the 1990 season, and it wasn't just a matter of waking up one day and saying "That's it." The fact was, Richard still loved to drive a race car. Maybe lying in a hospital bed after a wreck wasn't fun, but getting in the car and driving it on Sunday afternoons was.

"The burning desire wasn't like it had been ten years ago, but I still really, really enjoyed racing," Richard said.

"Still, there was other stuff to consider. Age

had something to do with it. Not winning races in so long had something to do with it. A lot of it came down to maybe that I was driving a lot different than I used to. Maybe I was not near as aggressive, thinking a little bit too much about what was going on instead of doing it. Stuff like that. So, I thought, 'Do I really need to keep doing this?'"

The answer was that he did not.

When Richard arrived at Daytona International Speedway in February for the 1991 Daytona 500, rumors were running hot and heavy that he had informed his primary sponsors, STP and Pontiac, of his intentions to retire. He had done just that, but Richard tried brushing aside the rumors when asked about them, just as he had done so many times in previous years.

Since those first rumors began showing up in the early '70s, Richard always told reporters that when the time came for him to announce retirement plans there would be no scoops. He would call everyone together and make the announcement to all at the same time.

He did that on October 1, 1991. The press conference at Petty Enterprises was attended by Richard's family, executives representing his many sponsors, politicians, and NASCAR officials.

Instead of saying simply, "That's it," as most members of his family, including Lynda, preferred, The King gave his many fans a year's notice of his forthcoming retirement. He would drive the full 1992 season, his 35th on the NASCAR circuit.

"It is not a farewell tour, because I won't be going anywhere after I get out of the car at the end of the '92 season," Richard said. "The deal is that I'll still be around as a car owner. The only difference will be that when I go to the tracks, I'll keep my cowboy hat on instead of putting my driver's helmet on."

Richard seemed more relieved than anything else after making the announcement. It was as if he had dumped a huge burden that had been weighing on him for a long time. He smiled as he remembered the good times, and he kept smiling when he talked about the long streak of winless seasons.

"Very few people enjoy doing what they do as much as I enjoy racing, or have had as much success in their profession," Richard said. "Just because I haven't won a race in such a long time, well, forget about that. I still had a lot of fun those years, being around the people and driving the car."

I could see Richard was at peace with himself and the decision that he was announcing. It wasn't easy, but I think he knew it was the right thing to do, and there would be no looking back, no second-guessing.

I was happy for him, and happy for his family. But there was a sadness, too. When Kyle Petty spoke about his father earlier that day he had predicted that a large part of the Richard Petty we knew would retire along with the driver's helmet. "The part of Richard Petty that you and I know and love will be put on the shelf somewhere and that will be a sad day," Kyle said. "When he gets out of the car and doesn't drive anymore, that will be a part of him we won't see anymore."

Everyone knew for a long time that the day was coming. Dale Inman, who was there from the start, knew it, but he still couldn't hold back a few tears.

A lot of others couldn't either.

RICHARD'S LAST DAYTONA 500

The time had arrived for Richard Petty, the driver, to begin saying farewell.

It was a warm, breezy, overcast morning at Daytona International Speedway when Richard arrived early for what would be his final Daytona 500 as a driver, and the first stop on his season-long Fan Appreciation Tour. Almost immediately he was surrounded by well-wishers and fans, holding out scraps of papers, pictures and programs for him to sign.

More fans awaited him in the garage area. He kept smiling and signing autographs as he slowly walked to the huge eighteen-wheel transport truck that serves as the team office and garage during race weeks.

Dale Inman and other crewman were busy making last-minute preparations to the shiny red and blue Pontiac.

Lee Petty sat on a work bench, smoking a pipe, alone with his thoughts. He greeted a few old friends, such as Junie Donlavey, a longtime team owner, who had been there when Richard

In his final Daytona 500, Richard was going to make history again. He was the Grand Marshal, so he would become the first driver ever to start the race in which he was competing.

began driving and had managed to hang in the sport without receiving much outside financial support.

The thing that struck me most as I drove through the camping areas outside of the speedway, through the tunnel entrance, and past the throng of fans in the infield on race morning was that the sport itself was ready to move past the Petty Era, which had its roots in those growing days when no promoter would think of running a race without Richard.

Richard was the center of attention throughout the 1992 SpeedWeek. Fans packed the shopping centers, purchasing everything they could find with Richard Petty's name or picture on it. And there was plenty to buy. They stood in long lines to get his autograph and a snapshot during his many personal appearances. Newspapers and magazines were full of stories and pictures about Richard.

But on race morning, it was evident those fans had come not only to pay respects to the end of a proud era and the man who once dominated it, but to cheer a new crowd of heroes, too, once the green-flag dropped.

The pennants and home-made banners flying from the campers and pickup trucks waved in support of Dale Earnhardt, Bill Elliott, Rusty Wallace, Bobby Allison's boy Davey, and Richard's son Kyle. The majority of those who chased Richard for an autograph wore T-shirts of other drivers.

I was reminded of some things Richard had said a few years earlier when I asked if he wished that he was just starting his career instead of nearing the end of it.

The only reason he could offer for wanting to do it again from the beginning was financial.

"If I was starting now, and had all the success that I had, I would have enough money for everyone in the garage to retire on," he said. "But the monetary deal is the only thing that might entice me to want to start all over again."

Selfishly, I had thought it would be great to see Richard Petty just starting his career, to turn back the years, and watch him bump fenders with Earnhardt or outfox Elliott in the draft for another Daytona 500 victory.

"But if we could do that, you would not know Richard Petty as you know Richard Petty now," he said. "In other words, the next thirty years in this sport is going to be unreal."

For those of us who traveled most of the previous thirty-year era with Richard, it already had become unreal.

The new breed of drivers seldom had time to sit and chat with fans or the media before or after the races. They were isolated by an army of public relations people, sponsor representatives, business agents and handlers.

Reporters were writing in-depth stories about drivers they didn't really know, using quotes fed to them from press releases.

In the good ol' days, Richard Petty was his own public relations man. He represented the factory or sponsors himself. He did his own business dealings, and he didn't need a personal handler to tell him what he should and shouldn't say.

Interviewing Richard was as simple as climbing up beside him in his tow truck, and beginning the conversation by asking how the kids were doing back home.

Those were the good ol' days. Richard Petty's good ol' days.

"I have seen them days, and I have been there," Richard said. "I have seen the growth of NASCAR, and no one is going to see the sport change as much as I have.

"I don't think you will ever see anyone dominate and stay on top as long as I did. It wasn't that I was so much better than everyone else. My organization was better. I drove for the same people most of them years, and we had a better organization because it was a family deal.

"Now is not the time to have a family organization in racing. Now you got to have an expert to do every single thing, a body man, a chassis man, an engine man.

"Used to be me, Maurice, Dale, and a couple of boys could do it all. You can't do that now. If I were starting out now, I couldn't be the individual that I was. You won't see that kind of stuff, someone driving his own car, again. It can't be done.

"When I came through this sport, it was Richard Petty's time to do it. Any other time would not have been Richard Petty's time."

Now, the clock had begun clicking down the minutes on Richard Petty's time, and some had said he already had stayed around too long, because he had not won a race since 1984. Old rival Bobby Allison was not among those.

"If Richard wants to stay out here forever and ride around behind the pace car, he has earned that right," Allison said.

Richard said it wasn't so much he had stayed beyond his time, but that he just had more time than he had good luck. "The Good Lord gave me twenty-five years of good luck, and I tried stretching it into thirty-five," he often said.

I laughed when Kyle Petty, grinning as always, left his father's truck on the morning of the 125-mile qualifying races complaining that Richard not only had used up all of his luck, but all of the family's luck, too.

"Neither one of us have had much good luck at Daytona lately," he said.

That didn't change in the qualifying races either.

I was standing near Richard's pit when I saw the caution flag come out. I immediately began looking at the string of cars coming down the front stretch, trying to spot the Number 43 Pontiac. A crewman got the bad news first over the two-way radio. He threw up his hands. "Right in front of him. There was nothing he could do," the crewman said.

The front of the Pontiac was smashed, and Richard was in the garage a short time later.

He explained that a couple of cars had spun,

and one had come down the track in front of him. "I just pushed him down through the grass and messed the front end all up," Richard said.

A few laps later, Kyle was another innocent victim when Dale Jarrett unintentionally slammed into his car.

Both Richard and Kyle had good qualifying speeds, so neither had to worry about not getting starting positions for the Daytona 500 after the bad luck in the qualifying race. Richard would start the 500 in the 32nd slot and Kyle in the 33rd.

Richard did not have much time Sunday morning to dwell on the fact that he was getting ready to run his final Daytona 500. He was honored with a new award presentation named in his honor during pre-race ceremonies. He and the other drivers rode around the track in convertibles during introductions. Richard got the biggest applause, and those with cameras tried to get a snapshot of him.

At the pre-race drivers meeting, Richard was besieged with requests for autographs. He signed and signed until, finally, Winston Cup director Dick Beaty pleaded for him to stop so the meeting could continue. Beaty explained to the drivers the procedure for the start of the race.

In his final Daytona 500, Richard was going to make history again. He was the Grand Marshal, so he would become the first driver ever to start the race in which he was competing. After giving the command, Richard was to move up from his starting spot and lead a ceremonial lap. Then he would drop back back to his 32nd starting position.

"Is someone gonna make sure he gets back to

where he is supposed to start?" Ken Schrader asked, jokingly.

Richard had it all figured out. "I am going to take a couple of laps before I give them other cats the signal to start their engines," he winked.

I watched as Richard walked to the starting line and prepared to crawl into his car. The crowd of people swirling around him didn't seem to bother him. He was smiling, saying hello, signing an autograph here and there. A small boy ran over to the edge of the crowd, poked his head through a tangle of arms and legs and ran back to his father with a big smile.

"You see him?" the father asked.

The little boy nodded. "I saw Richard," he said excitedly.

The father stood on tip-toes and stretched his neck. "He looks a little older than on television," he said.

The fans were shooed away as the drivers entered their cars and crewmen began attaching the steering wheels and fastening safety belts. It was time for Richard to get this show on the road, but there would be none of this 'Gentlemen, start your engines' stuff from The King.

"Okay, guys, let's go. Crank 'em up," Richard said simply.

If the prayers and dreams of thousands of race fans had been answered, Richard Petty would have given Ol' Blue the gas, shifted into high gear, and ridden the high banks for a story-book victory.

This was not a day for miracles. Instead, it was a good, solid performance that left Richard and the rest of the Petty clan feeling proud and satisfied, everything considered.

After another bout of bad luck – he was caught in the multi-car wreck on the 97th lap that eliminated several contenders – Richard came back with a strong run to finish 16th, two laps behind winner Davey Allison.

"We didn't get what we wanted, but I guess Davey was the only one who did that," Richard allowed. "I wish we had done better. The big deal was if we could have run all day and not had any trouble we could have had a good finish. But circumstances weren't on our side for me to run a trouble-free race."

In 1991 Richard had been singled out unfairly by one writer for being involved in so many wrecks. Richard let it be known that he was a victim of circumstances during the wreck on Lap 97. He was coming off the second turn when he saw puffs of smoke and cars breaking out of line. He let off the throttle to avoid the trouble and got popped from behind.

"So, you can't say 'Richard Petty had a wreck.' Somebody put Richard Petty in a wreck and totaled his car out. He didn't run into anybody. They run into him," he emphasized.

Lynda Petty, who watched the race on television from a bus in the infield, had rushed to greet her husband as he brought the car back to the garage following the end of the race. "I am so excited and thrilled that we finished the race," Lynda exclaimed.

Richard was surrounded by reporters, photographers and well-wishers as he slid through the window of the car, removed his helmet and quickly put on his cowboy hat and sunglasses.

He looked at the car. He grimaced a bit, and then he smiled, the way I had seen him do hundreds of times previously. I could tell it had not yet struck Richard that he had just completed his final Daytona 500.

Over in Victory Lane, once The King's castle, Bobby Allison's son Davey was celebrating his first Daytona 500 victory. It was the second time the event had been won by a former winner's son. The only other time was in 1964 when Richard joined his father, Lee, as a Daytona 500 winner.

Davey knew he would never win 200 races, and perhaps not another six Daytona 500s. "But it sure feels good to know that I've done one of the things that Richard did," Davey said. "He is a good man. A good champion. And he was great competition for my dad."

That was a special memory Davey had to take home with him, along with the victory trophy, from Richard Petty's final Daytona 500.

Those of us who were fortunate enough to stand watch on Richard Petty's time, the best of times, had our memories too, of the man we always would remember as, The King.

THE RECORD BOOK

A complete list of Richard Petty's wins

1960

Date	Track	Miles	Money won	Make of car
February 28	Charlotte, NC	100	800	Plymouth
April 10	Martinsville, VA	250	3,340	Plymouth
September 19	Hillsborough, NC	99	800	Plymouth

1961

Date	Track	Miles	Money won	Make of car
April 23	Richmond, VA	100	950	Plymouth
May 21	Charlotte, NC	100	800	Plymouth

1962

Date	Track	Miles	Money won	Make of car
April 15	North Wilkesboro, NC	250	2,275	Plymouth
April 22	Martinsville, VA	250	3,400	Plymouth
July 14	Greenville, SC	100	1,000	Plymouth
August 8	Huntsville, AL	50	580	Plymouth
August 15	Roanoke, VA	50	550	Plymouth
August 18	Winston-Salem, NC	50	600	Plymouth
August 21	Spartanburg, SC	100	1,000	Plymouth
September 30	North Wilkesboro, NC	200	2,560	Plymouth
November 1	Tampa, FL	67	780	Plymouth

1963

Date	Track	Miles	Money won	Make of car
March 2	Spartanburg, SC	100	1,000	Plymouth
March 3	Weaverville, NC	100	1,000	Plymouth
April 14	South Boston, VA	150	1,500	Plymouth
April 21	Martinsville, VA	250	3,375	Plymouth
April 28	North Wilkesboro, NC	250	3,575	Plymouth
May 2	Columbia, SC	100	1,000	Plymouth
May 18	Manassas, VA	112	1,000	Plymouth
June 9	Birmingham, AL	100	1,000	Plymouth
July 21	Bridgehampton, NY	100	1,000	Plymouth
July 30	Greenville, SC	100	1,000	Plymouth
August 8	Columbia, SC	100	1,140	Plymouth
October 5	Randleman, NC	50	580	Plymouth
October 20	South Boston, VA	150	1,550	Plymouth
December 29	Savannah, GA	100	1,000	Plymouth

1964

Date	Track	Miles	Money won	Make of car
February 23	Daytona, FL	500	33,300	Plymouth
May 17	South Boston, VA	100	1,000	Plymouth
June 11	Concord, NC	100	1,000	Plymouth
June 14	Nashville, TN	100	1,000	Plymouth
June 26	Spartanburg, SC	100	1,000	Plymouth
August 2	Nashville, TN	200	2,150	Plymouth
August 16	Huntington, WV	219	2,550	Plymouth
October 25	Harris, NC	100	1,000	Plymouth

1965

Date	Track	Miles	Money won	Make of car
July 31	Nashville, TN	200	2,350	Plymouth
August 8	Weaverville, NC	250	3,200	Plymouth

September 10	Hickory, NC	100	1,200	Plymouth
September 17	Manassas, VA	150	2,300	Plymouth
November 14	Augusta, GA	150	1,700	Plymouth

1966

Date	Track	Miles	Money won	Make of car
February 22	Daytona, FL	500	28,150	Plymouth
April 30	Darlington, SC	400	12,115	Plymouth
May 7	Hampton, VA	100	1,000	Plymouth
May 10	Macon, GA	100	1,000	Plymouth
May 12	Weaverville, NC	150	1,400	Plymouth
July 30	Nashville, TN	200	2,750	Plymouth
August 7	Atlanta, GA	400	13,525	Plymouth
November 13	Augusta, GA	150	1,735	Plymouth

1967

Date	Track	Miles	Money won	Make of car
March 5	Weaverville, NC	150	1,800	Plymouth
April 6	Columbia, SC	100	1,000	Plymouth
April 9	Hickory, NC	100	1,000	Plymouth
April 23	Martinsville, VA	250	4,450	Plymouth
April 30	Richmond, VA	125	2,150	Plymouth
May 13	Darlington, SC	400	14,090	Plymouth
May 20	Hampton, VA	100	1,000	Plymouth
June 6	Macon, GA	150	1,400	Plymouth
June 8	Maryville, TN	100	1,000	Plymouth
June 18	Rockingham, NC	500	16,175	Plymouth
June 24	Greenville, SC	100	1,000	Plymouth
July 9	Trenton, NJ	300	4,350	Plymouth
July 13	Fonda, NY	100	1,150	Plymouth
July 15	Islip, NY	60	1,150	Plymouth

July 23	Bristol, TN	250	6,050	Plymouth
July 29	Nashville, TN	200	2,050	Plymouth
August 12	Winston-Salem, NC	62	1,000	Plymouth
August 17	Columbia, SC	100	1,000	Plymouth
August 25	Savannah, GA	100	1,000	Plymouth
September 4	Darlington, SC	500	26,900	Plymouth
September 8	Hickory, NC	100	1,500	Plymouth
September 10	Richmond, VA	150	2,450	Plymouth
September 15	Beltsville, MD	150	1,400	Plymouth
September 17	Hillsborough, NC	150	1,500	Plymouth
September 24	Martinsville, VA	250	4,400	Plymouth
October 1	North Wilkesboro, NC	250	4,725	Plymouth
November 6	Montgomery, AL	100	1,200	Plymouth

1968

Date	Track	Miles	Money won	Make of car
April 7	Hickory, NC	100	1,200	Plymouth
April 13	Greenville, SC	100	1,200	Plymouth
May 41	Asheville, NC	100	1,200	Plymouth
June 6	Maryville, TN	100	1,200	Plymouth
June 8	Birmingham, AL	100	1,200	Plymouth
June 22	Greenville, SC	100	1,200	Plymouth
July 9	Oxford, ME	100	1,350	Plymouth
July 11	Fonda, NY	100	1,200	Plymouth
July 25	Maryville, TN	100	1,200	Plymouth
August 23	South Boston, VA	100	1,200	Plymouth
September 8	Richmond, VA	187	2,400	Plymouth
September 15	Hillsborough, NC	150	1,600	Plymouth
September 22	Martinsville, VA	250	5,999	Plymouth
September 29	North Wilkesboro, NC	250	5,975	Plymouth
October 27	Rockingham, NC	500	17,075	Plymouth
November 17	Macon, GA	250	3,500	Plymouth

1969

Date	Track	Miles	Money won	Make of car
February 1	Riverside, CA	500	19,650	Ford
April 1	Martinsville, VA	250	10,275	Ford
June 19	Kingsport, TN	100	1,000	Ford
July 6	Dover, DE	300	4,725	Ford
July 15	Beltsville, MD	150	2,500	Ford
July 26	Nashville, TN	200	3,000	Ford
July 27	Maryville, TN	100	1,000	Ford
August 22	Winston-Salem, NC	62	1,000	Ford
August 28	Martinsville, VA	250	10,085	Ford

1970

Date	Track	Miles	Money won	Make of car
March 8	Rockingham, NC	500	16,715	Plymouth
March 15	Savannah, GA	100	1,000	Plymouth
April 18	North Wilkesboro, NC	250	6,025	Plymouth
April 30	Columbia, SC	100	1,500	Plymouth
June 14	Riverside, CA	400	18,840	Plymouth
June 26	Kingsport, TN	100	1,500	Plymouth
July 7	Malta, NY	90	1,500	Plymouth
July 12	Trenton, NJ	300	6,730	Plymouth
July 24	Maryville, TN	104	1,500	Plymouth
August 2	Atlanta, GA	500	19,600	Plymouth
August 11	Ona, WV	131	1,700	Plymouth
August 28	Winston-Salem, NC	62	1,000	Plymouth
August 29	South Boston, VA	100	1,500	Plymouth
September 13	Richmond, VA	271	4,675	Plymouth
September 20	Dover, DE	300	6,195	Plymouth
September 30	Raleigh, NC	100	1,000	Plymouth
October 18	Martinsville, VA	262	8,775	Plymouth
November 8	Macon, GA	274	3,275	Plymouth

1971

Date	Track	Miles	Money won	Make of car
February 14	Daytona, FL	500	45,450	Plymouth
March 7	Richmond, VA	271	4,425	Plymouth
March 14	Rockingham, NC	500	17,315	Plymouth
March 21	Hickory, NC	100	2,200	Plymouth
April 8	Columbia, SC	100	1,700	Plymouth
April 15	Maryville, TN	104	1,000	Plymouth
April 18	North Wilkesboro, NC	250	4,545	Plymouth
April 25	Martinsville, VA	250	5,075	Plymouth
May 21	Asheville, NC	100	1,500	Plymouth
June 26	Greenville, SC	100	1,500	Plymouth
July 14	Malta, NY	90	1,500	Plymouth
July 15	Islip, NY	50	1,500	Plymouth
July 18	Trenton, NJ	300	6,760	Plymouth
July 24	Nashville, TN	250	4,325	Plymouth
August 1	Atlanta, GA	500	20,220	Plymouth
August 8	Ona, WV	219	2,300	Plymouth
August 27	Columbia, SC	100	1,500	Plymouth
October 17	Dover, DE	500	14,570	Plymouth
October 24	Rockingham, NC	500	17,120	Plymouth
November 14	Richmond, VA	271	4,450	Plymouth
December 12	College Station, TX	500	13,395	Plymouth

1972

Date	Track	Miles	Money won	Make of car
January 23	Riverside, CA	500	18,170	STP-Plymouth
February 27	Richmond, VA	271	5,300	STP-Plymouth
April 23	North Wilkesboro, NC	250	6,600	STP-Plymouth
April 30	Martinsville, VA	263	8,250	STP-Plymouth
June 25	College Station, TX	500	16,245	STP-Plymouth
September 10	Richmond, VA	217	6,775	STP-Plymouth

| September 24 | Martinsville, VA | 262 | 7,350 | STP-Plymouth |
| October 1 | North Wilkesboro, NC | 250 | 7,200 | STP-Plymouth |

1973

Date	Track	Miles	Money won	Make of car
February 18	Daytona, FL	500	36,100	STP-Dodge
February 25	Richmond, VA	271	6,350	STP-Dodge
April 8	North Wilkesboro, NC	250	6,230	STP-Dodge
June 10	College Station, TX	500	17,820	STP-Dodge
September 9	Richmond, VA	271	6,775	STP-Dodge
September 30	Martinsville, VA	262	11,750	STP-Dodge

1974

Date	Track	Miles	Money won	Make of car
February 17	Daytona, FL	450	39,650	STP-Dodge
March 3	Rockingham, NC	450	18,025	STP-Dodge
April 21	North Wilkesboro, NC	225	8,250	STP-Dodge
May 12	Nashville, TN	238	7,900	STP-Dodge
June 16	Brooklyn MI	360	17,190	STP-Dodge
July 28	Hampton, GA	500	19,350	STP-Dodge
August 4	Pocono, PA	500	17,000	STP-Dodge
August 11	Talladega, AL	500	24,465	STP-Dodge
September 8	Richmond, VA	271	8,740	STP-Dodge
September 15	Dover, DE	500	18,175	STP-Dodge

1975

Date	Track	Miles	Money won	Make of car
February 23	Richmond, VA	271	8,265	STP-Dodge
March 16	Bristol, TN	266	7,350	STP-Dodge
March 23	Atlanta, GA	500	19,500	STP-Dodge

April 6	North Wilkesboro, NC	250	8,675	STP-Dodge
April 27	Martinsville, VA	262	20,000	STP-Dodge
May 25	Charlotte, NC	600	30,290	STP-Dodge
June 8	Riverside, CA	400	18,135	STP-Dodge
July 4	Daytona, FL	400	19,935	STP-Dodge
August 24	Brooklyn, MI	400	18,140	STP-Dodge
September 14	Dover, DE	500	18,250	STP-Dodge
September 21	North Wilkesboro, NC	250	9,960	STP-Dodge
October 5	Charlotte, NC	500	30,970	STP-Dodge
November 2	Bristol, TN	266	7,560	STP-Dodge

1976

Date	Track	Miles	Money won	Make of car
February 29	Rockingham, NC	500	19,915	STP-Dodge
August 1	Long Pond, PA	500	20,640	STP-Dodge
October 24	Rockingham, NC	500	20,395	STP-Dodge

1977

Date	Track	Miles	Money won	Make of car
March 13	Rockingham, NC	500	18,594	STP-Dodge
March 20	Hampton, GA	500	22,550	STP-Dodge
May 29	Charlotte, NC	600	69,500	STP-Dodge
June 12	Riverside, CA	249	18,255	STP-Dodge
July 4	Daytona, FL	400	23,075	STP-Dodge

1979

Date	Track	Miles	Money won	Make of car
February 18	Daytona, FL	500	73,900	STP-Oldsmobile
April 22	Martinsville, VA	262	23,400	STP-Chevrolet
August 19	Brooklyn, MI	400	21,100	STP-Chevrolet

| September 16 | Dover, DE | 500 | 21,650 | STP-Chevrolet |
| October 21 | Rockingham, NC | 500 | 20,960 | STP-Chevrolet |

1980

Date	Track	Miles	Money won	Make of car
April 20	North Wilkesboro, NC	250	18,925	STP-Chevrolet
May 10	Nashville, TN	250	15,350	STP-Chevrolet

1981

Date	Track	Miles	Money won	Make of car
February 15	Daytona, FL	500	90,575	STP-Buick
April 5	North Wilkesboro, NC	250	18,850	STP-Buick
August 16	Brooklyn, MI	400	23,750	STP-Buick

1983

Date	Track	Miles	Money won	Make of car
March 13	Rockingham, NC	500	24,150	STP-Pontiac
May 1	Talladega, AL	500	46,650	STP-Pontiac
October 9	Charlotte, NC	500	40,400	STP-Pontiac

1984

Date	Track	Miles	Money won	Make of car
May 20	Dover, DE	500	28,105	STP-Pontiac
July 4	Daytona, FL	400	43,755	STP-Pontiac